What's Your Love I.Q.?

— To which female country music legend is Jennifer Love Hewitt related?
— Which famous Mattel doll gave JLH her big break in commercials?
— What movie was made from an idea JLH received in a dream?
— What video features songs which are all sung by Jennifer Love Hewitt?
— Where did fifteen-year-old JLH get her first kiss, and from whom?
— Which male star makes Jennifer go totally ga-ga?
— How many injuries did JLH get by doing most of her own stunts in *I Know What You Did Last Summer*?
— What will Jennifer never, ever do in a movie?

Find all the answers,
and much more, inside . . .

Jennifer Love Hewitt

ANNA LOUISE GOLDEN

St. Martin's Paperbacks

NOTE: If you purchased this book without a cover you should be aware that this book is stolen property. It was reported as "unsold and destroyed" to the publisher, and neither the author nor the publisher has received any payment for this "stripped book."

JENNIFER LOVE HEWITT

Copyright © 1999 by Anna Louise Golden.

Cover photograph by Barry King/Liaison Agency.

All rights reserved. No part of this book may be used or reproduced in any manner whatsoever without written permission except in the case of brief quotations embodied in critical articles or reviews. For information address St. Martin's Press, 175 Fifth Avenue, New York, N.Y. 10010.

ISBN: 0-312-96991-0

Printed in the United States of America

St. Martin's Paperbacks edition/May 1999

10 9 8 7 6 5 4 3 2 1

FOR TASHA, JUST BECAUSE . . .

Acknowledgments

As always, my agent, Madeleine Morel, is da bomb. And so is my editor, Glenda Howard, who knows that JLH rocks. Stephanie Ogle, at Cinema Books in Seattle, was incredibly helpful, as she always is. My mum and dad have always believed in me, and maybe it took a while, but I think it's finally paid off. A bunch of friends lent support, tangible and otherwise, so many, many thanks to Mike M., Dennis, Paul and Cathy, Kevan (even if he is a Liverpool supporter), the G&D crew, and probably lots more I haven't mentioned. You know who you are and how you relate to ALG. Last, but never, ever least, L&G, with more thanks and love than you know. And the DigiHippie at *Teen People*. Ta.

The following pieces were invaluable for putting this book together: "Love of the Party" by Dennis Hensley, *Movieline*, June 1998. *E! Online* Q&A with Jennifer Love Hewitt. "Jennifer Love Hewitt Finds Stardom Worth the Wait" by Jose Martinez, MSNBS. *TotalTV*, "Heart to Heat" by Judith Maitland. *Entertainment Tonight Online*, "JLH". *Sun Herald Online*, "Hewitt Takes Up the Torch for Teens in Film" by Mal Vincent. *Southam Newspapers*, "Typical Teen Wannabe" by Jamie Portman. *Soap Opera Update*, "Party Girl" by Damon Romine. *Tribute*, "Love Conquers All" by Andrew Ryan. "No Ordinary Love" by Stephen Saban,

Detour, June/July 1998. "Love Can't Wait" by Rosie Amodio, *YM,* July 1998. *AOL Online Chats with Jennifer Love Hewitt,* 1996 and 1997. *TV Gen Online Chat,* October 15, 1997. "Fresh Faces," *WWD,* March 13, 1998. "Soulful Musings," by Julie Jordan, *People,* September 29, 1997. *E!Online,* Star Boards. "Love Horrors," *Entertainment Weekly,* November 7, 1997. *E!Online,* Sizzlin' Sixteen. *People Online,* cover story, April 21, 1997. "Scream Queens" by Jeanne Rohrer, *Femme Fatale,* April 1998. *TNT's Rough Cut. TV Gen,* Listen Up with Jennifer Love Hewitt. "Jennifer Love Hewitt," by Monica Rizzo, *Teen People,* February 1998. "Party Girl," by Pam Lambert, *People,* September 23, 1996. "Can't Hardly Miss" by Eric Layton, *Entertainment Today.* "Hewitt a Nerd," by Steve Tilley, *Edmonton Sun.* "No Pain, No Gain," by Joshua Mooney, *Movieline,* March 1998. "Love Connection," by Nina Malkin, *Teen,* May 1998. "Party Till You Drop," by Eliza Bergman Krause, *Seventeen,* May 1998. *Party of Five: The Unofficial Companion,* by Brenda Scott Royce, Renaissance Books, 1997.

Introduction

Call her Love. Everyone does, and if a name ever suited anyone, Love suits her. She's sweet, funny, a total babe who can dance, sing and, oh yeah, act.

She's been in show business since she was a little kid; it's as if she were born just to do all this. And she does it very, very well. How many people could be on one of the coolest shows on television *and* in one of the hottest movies of the nineties, while releasing three CDs? Very few. Love has got it down.

Most people in her position would be thinking of themselves as big stars. They'd want the treatment: limos, the best of everything, dinner at fancy restaurants. They'd want to be seen at all the fashionable parties in clothes from all the top designers. They'd be expected to hang out, to be seen. That's the way Hollywood works.

But Love isn't most people. She only got her driver's license recently (okay, she owns a Land Rover Discovery, but what the hey, she's earned some luxury). She still lives with her mom, not at some swank address in Beverly Hills, but in an apartment in Burbank. You're not going to find her at the Polo Lounge or shopping on Rodeo Drive; you're much more likely to run into her at McDonald's or looking for clothes at the mall. In other words, her feet are very, very firmly planted on the ground.

As Sarah Reeves on *Party of Five,* she's been nothing less than brilliant. The role, the whole show, has been intense, lurching from crisis to crisis but rewarding in every way. Because of that part, she ended up being cast in *I Know What You Did Last Summer,* Kevin Williamson's continued foray into teen horror flicks, and one that astonished everyone by taking in more than $71 million at the box office. Not bad for a piece of fluff. But it hit a chord, and as Julie James, Love hit an even bigger chord.

And that was how she won the part as the star of *Can't Hardly Wait,* why she'll be the star (along with Brandy and Freddie Prinze, Jr., the only other returning member of the cast) of *I Still Know What You Did Last Summer.* It's also, in part, why she can come up with an idea in a dream, scribble it down while flying on an airplane, and suddenly find herself writing, co-producing, and starring in yet another film (she also plans on being involved in the soundtrack—if that's not hands-on, nothing is), *Cupid's Love.* Not many nineteen-year-olds can do that.

Then again, Love is far from being most nineteen-year-olds. Most girls her age haven't been all over the world, or starred in ads on television. They're not on their fourth TV series. They're not driven the way Love is. When others were content to just go to school, she says, "I was kinda like, 'Don't you want to do more with your life? You're fourteen, get a job!' I don't know which was more the freak, me or them."

These days, no one is going to think of Love as a freak. When she was young, growing up in Texas, she was certainly different, entering beauty pageants, singing and dancing, and finally convincing her mom that she wanted to try life in showbiz, in Los Angeles—a pretty big decision for a ten-year-old.

Her enthusiasm and dedication were so great, though, that her mom was willing to give up her own career and give it a try. So Love and her mother packed up and headed west.

Some things, perhaps, are meant to be, and Love Hewitt (the name she went by in those days) was meant to be in show business, and in California. Within a month she was working; within a year she was on her first series, Disney's *Kids Incorporated*.

She's never regretted leaving Texas, and leaving her past. But why should she? Her life couldn't have turned out better if it had been a story. It almost *is* a story, in many ways: small-town girl, eager and talented, comes to the big, bad city and wins it over until she's a major, major star, but still the sweet girl she'd always been. But if it had happened that way in a movie, no one would have believed it.

And, like any story, there's a happy ending, with Love moving from project to project, a totally hot Hollywood commodity. And until recently, there was also a knight in shining armor—or at least its modern equivalent driving a BMW. In this case it's Will Friedle, the star of the TV sitcom *Boy Meets World*. In classic fashion, he was literally the boy next door—okay, actually the boy across the street—but that just fit in perfectly with the type of boyfriend Jennifer Love Hewitt would have. Someone as down-to-earth as herself, not looking for the big time, but happy with who he is—and who she is. After two years together, though, it all fell apart, and Love was back on the dating trail, falling into the arms of MTV hunk Carson Daly.

You're not going to find Love at too many big Hollywood parties—you'd have a better chance searching for her at craft stores. This is someone who'll hang out at paint-your-own ceramic stores, and actually do the painting herself, or make boxes and photo albums to give to friends or even sell.

She may not be comfortable with the idea of being a "star," but she knows it's real, and that with it come a lot of responsibilities. Like it or not, she's a role model, and if she has to be one, then she'll do it properly. So she works very actively with Big Sisters, and Tuesday's Child, a pediatric AIDS organization, and she's even on the advisory board of *Teen People,* a position she takes very seriously.

Everything's come together perfectly for Jennifer Love Hewitt, her life, her career, her dreams. It's as if she has the golden touch, and the gilt doesn't seem to be fading. In part because of her costume in *I Know What You Did Last Summer* she's even become something she never expected: a sex symbol, a major babe.

"I kind of shocked myself watching it," she admitted.

She doesn't aim to be a sex symbol. She doesn't aim to be anything but the very best she can be at anything she undertakes. Naturally modest, she understands that there's been a lot of effort and a lot of luck involved in her rise to the top.

She's more than happy to give a lot of the credit to her mother, Pat, "my best friend—my older sister and my mother all at the same time." And she's more than happy to keep sharing the Burbank apartment with Pat, even though she's old enough, and definitely mature enough, to handle living alone.

Jennifer Love Hewitt has become one of a growing number of young actresses who can move easily between the small and large screens, and make a big impact in both. Like her *Party of Five* colleague Neve Campbell or Sarah Michelle Gellar of *Buffy the Vampire Slayer* she's at home in both worlds, although, unlike Neve—at least, if the rumors are to be believed—Love has absolutely no desire to leave *PO5* for a more glittering career in the movies.

Love knows quite well that without the exposure she's received as Sarah Reeves on *Party of Five,* she might not have had many of the opportunities that have come her way since. Being seen all over America every Wednesday night, appearing on the teen psychodrama, has made her into a household name for more than one generation.

"I love *Party of Five*," she said. "It's the best job I ever had. Without [it] I would not be doing all the stuff I'm getting to do now. It's the greatest show in the world, and I'm holding on to it as long as possible, because I know there will never, ever be another show like it."

There certainly hasn't been one that's gone through as many crises, both on and off the screen. Not only are the relationships tortured, but its near-cancellation, thwarted by a concerted campaign on the part of viewers, also has meant that it has a special place in the hearts of a lot of people. That includes Love, although she'd hardly seen the show before she was asked to audition for Sarah (up until then her time had been occupied in central Oregon, far from any urban center, working on another series).

These days, in part because of the strengths she's shown as Sarah and as Julie James, Love has become something of a role model herself. While she understands that it's her *characters* who are really the role models, not her, she admits that "I like being a role model. I definitely won't do a film that I feel would teach somebody that looks up to me something they shouldn't be doing. But I wouldn't really do those films anyway—it's not me."

Sarah, in particular, has been shown to be all too human; she makes mistakes, "and there isn't a person in the universe who doesn't make mistakes," Love says.

Love's career has come into its own at the perfect time. Girls really are coming to the forefront again. People are taking them seriously once more. And Love is at the very head of a generation that's making all that happen. Some people might dismiss "Girl Power" as a

Spice Girls cliché, but it's very, very real. And it's very important. It's about respect, the respect of others and respect for yourself.

"I think it's now at its best," Love explained. "Other generations weren't taught self-respect and strength until something came along to jeopardize [women]. But in my generation, we're taught that the most important thing is to respect yourself. Just because you wear high heels in the evening doesn't mean that you can't wear tennis shoes during the day and kick some major butt in the business world and do really amazing, powerful things."

It's a change that's happening in part due to girls like Love. What she does, the way she behaves on the screen, has an effect on her fans. They love her for the strength she shows, the decisions she makes.

In turn, Love knows she owes a great deal to those fans.

"I go into their living rooms every Wednesday night, and I say, 'Like me, like me, like me. Be my friend, be my friend.' And then to expect them to come up to me in public and have me say no would be ridiculous."

As much as she's a role model, Jennifer Love Hewitt can still be a fan. She's the girl who collects autographs of all the famous people she meets, who still has a crush on Johnny Depp (who sent her flowers for her graduation and actually came to the *Party of Five* set to meet her once).

She's on the boundary between girl and woman, with bits of both coloring her outlook on the world. She has a very strong sense of who she is, and the things that are important to her, a true moral compass to help guide her. Don't ever expect any nude scenes—they're simply not going to happen. She might be willing to wear a sexy costume, to be "eye candy" as she puts it, but nothing more than that. No exploitation.

Jennifer Love Hewitt has done her growing up on the

soundstage, in front of the camera. From the age of ten, that's where she's been, following her dream. She's found that dream now, and she's discovered along the way that, really, it's just one part of life, nothing more. There are plenty of things beyond acting, even beyond singing. She's found out truths that some people go their entire lives without realizing. She's a remarkable young woman. Then again, she's had a remarkable young life . . .

Chapter One

Texas is unlike anywhere else in the United States. It's where the old ways of the South meet the can-do bustle of the Southwest. It's the largest state in the continental U.S., with two big cities, Dallas in the north and Houston in the south, as its major urban centers.

More than anything, Texas is fiercely independent. They do things their way, and always have done, from the Alamo onward. To say you're a Texan means you're a little different from the rest of the U.S.

While Texas is completely a part of the modern age, the number of small towns and cities that cover the state means that many of the values hark back a little further, to the time when small towns were the norm, and the idea of the city actually scared a lot of people. High school football still inspires terrific loyalties in Texas, even among adults. Beauty pageants, which so many people in the big cities see as something out of the past, remain an important part of small-town Texan life. It's America past and present.

Killeen is about as close to the center of Texas as any city. The closest big city is Austin, the great Texan anomaly—a college town, very forward-thinking and one of America's music centers. Killeen is where Jennifer Love Hewitt grew up.

She was actually born just a few miles farther north, in Waco (a town which would become notorious in

1994 for the confrontation between law officers and members of the Branch Davidian sect), on February 21, 1979.

Her parents, Pat and Tom Hewitt, already had one child, a son named Todd, who was eight years old when his sister was born. As soon as she knew she was going to give birth to a girl, Pat Hewitt was certain of the name she wanted for her daughter: Love.

"I was named after my mom's best friend in college, who's like five eleven, long blond hair past her butt, big blue eyes, freckles, and an hourglass figure," Jennifer Love explained. "She was the most beautiful woman my mom had ever seen, and they were so close. My mom said if she ever had a little girl, she would name her Love, so when I was born of course she named me Love—even though I came out, like, five three, brown hair, half an hourglass figure, and completely different looking."

That seemed like a good enough reason, but there was another: "My lips were heart-shaped when I was born, according to my mom." It was somehow inevitable that the girl would be named Love.

Love would have been her only first name, if it hadn't been for brother Todd. At eight, he understood just how a girl who was named Love was going to be teased in Texas. It didn't matter how great the name was, or what attachment it had in his mother's memory, you just didn't do that to a kid there. He suggested that Love be the baby's middle name, and that she have a normal first name.

On consideration, his parents realized that their son was right. Their way of thanking him was to let him choose his sister's first name—quite an honor for an eight-year-old. Jennifer was the one that came to mind, mostly because he had a crush on a girl called Jennifer, who lived just down the street from the Hewitt house.

So, when the child came into the world, Jennifer

Love Hewitt was the name she was known by—and Love to all her family and friends.

One thing nobody anticipated was that she'd become a performer of any kind. There was no history of that in the family—at least, not in the immediate family. If you were to branch out a little, you'd find that her grandmother's third cousin had been the late country-music singing legend, Patsy Cline. But that hardly seemed to count, it was so far removed.

All the ingredients for a perfect family were there: two parents, a son, and a lovely baby daughter. But it wasn't in the cards. Barely six months after Jennifer Love was born, Pat and Tom Hewitt divorced.

The children, of course, stayed with their mother, who needed a good job to support them. In college she'd received her degree in speech pathology, and she was able to find work in her field not far away, just down the road in Killeen. The town did have some advantages; it was a good place to raise kids, it was relatively cheap, and it was a little closer to the cultural center of Austin. For Todd, who was old enough to have a set of friends in Waco, it meant adjusting to a new place, a new school, and making a whole new set of friends. As for Jennifer, she might as well never have lived anywhere else.

As soon as the little girl could walk, she did everything she could to get attention. And once she began talking, the spotlight was all that she craved. She'd sing, dance, talk. If there were visitors at the house, she'd want to entertain them. Pat might have wondered where all this came from, but she accepted it as a part of her daughter's personality, figuring it was a phase she'd probably grow out of soon enough.

The months passed, and Jennifer Love *didn't* grow out of it. She continued to take every opportunity she could find to entertain, to be the center of attention with her singing and her dancing. It was, it seemed, simply something that was a part of her, and her family had better get used to it. Who knew where it would all lead?

One thing Pat Hewitt was not was a showbiz mother. She encouraged her daughter to express herself, but she wasn't the type to immediately start dragging her little girl to auditions, agents, and beauty pageants as soon as she began craving the spotlight. She had no stage ambitions of her own to project onto her daughter. She'd support her all she could, if that was what the girl really wanted to do, but she wasn't going to push her in any direction. Let her grow up for herself. Maybe it *would* all turn out to be a phase she was going through.

If Pat ever really believed that, the notion changed completely when Love was three. The family was out at a dinner club. Suddenly Pat and Todd, who was then eleven years old, discovered that Love was missing. She wasn't at the table, or under it, and they couldn't see her anywhere in the room. Panicked, they began searching frantically, until Pat heard a familiar voice in another room. There was Jennifer, perched very cutely on top of a baby grand piano, and while the accompanist played, she sang Kris Kristofferson's "Help Me Make It Through the Night," to the great enjoyment of the people sitting at the tables.

At that moment Pat probably realized that it was all a lost cause, that her daughter was destined to have a life on the stage. If she was going to become an entertainer, though, she had to do it the right way. So when Love was four, her mother enrolled her in dancing lessons. Before she'd even reached kindergarten, she could tap!

Love didn't think of her dinner club performance as her public debut, however. That came a little later.

"I started singing songs off the radio when I was three and four, and did my first live singing performance when I was six," she recalled.

Everyone has to start somewhere, and for Jennifer Love Hewitt (or Love Hewitt, as she was still called back then), it was at a fair, one of those institutions that still play an important part in the life of smaller towns in America. The kind of affair where people and livestock are of equal importance, as Love would quickly find out. She'd been booked to sing, and arrived with her mother, only to discover that until an hour before, her venue had been housing pigs—they'd had to clear them out so she could perform.

It wasn't Carnegie Hall, or the Hollywood Bowl, but that didn't matter. She was able to get up on a stage, to appear in the spotlight, and to entertain—the things she instinctively felt she'd been made to do. There was some singing, and some dancing, the opportunity to show off all her talents.

That was the beginning, and having had a taste, Love wanted more—a lot more. She'd perform anywhere she could—county fairs, livestock shows—anyplace that would have her. In fact, her first "real" performance was at that "livestock show in a pig barn, [where] I sang Whitney Houston's 'The Greatest Love of All,' and there was a talent scout there," she recalled. The scout recognized that Love was a very precocious talent. Not only was she cute, but she could really sing—and dance. He recommended to Pat that she do everything she could to encourage her daughter and let her develop her talent with lessons, exposure, every way she could. Soon she began to take part in the junior beauty pageants that were—and still are—very popular in Texas, and her charm and quite obvious talent won her the title of "living doll."

As she did more and more, and began thinking of herself as a performer, she began to realize just how different she was from the friends she had in Killeen.

"I never really fit in where I lived in Texas. I would host and direct and star in these little plays, and my friends never really wanted to do it. I thought there was something wrong with them."

It was typical that she wouldn't think of herself as the odd one. From the very beginning, Love had had a tremendous amount of confidence and certainty about what she was doing. It all seemed so right for her, so how could she be strange?

Besides, all she had to do was turn on her television, and she could see other kids entertaining. When she was young, her favorite show was NBC's *Punky Brewster,* with the young Soleil Moon Frye in the title role. She wasn't much older than Love, and there she was, going into millions of homes every week. How could a desire to entertain be so strange when so many people could watch you? Lots of people did it, there was nothing weird about it. What seemed strange to Jennifer was the way others seemed happy to just play or do absolutely nothing. She wanted to keep her time filled, to make people happy, to make them smile.

"I'd watch Punky Brewster and I wanted to be her. I didn't know what she was, I didn't know it was called acting. I just knew I wanted to be her, that I could do her part."

All Jennifer's activities were exhausting for Pat. She drove her to the fairs and pageants, made sure everything was fine, and stayed to watch and support her daughter. But she was a single parent who also had a teenage son to deal with, as well as her own career. Pat Hewitt was doing well as a speech therapist in Killeen, making the money she needed to support her family. Although she never seemed to have any time to herself, that was fine; she certainly couldn't complain that her life was empty!

One thing she insisted on was that Jennifer keep up her dance classes. She'd shown herself to be a very talented dancer, and with an early start, she could possibly succeed in the dance field.

As part of her classes, Jennifer had to participate in dance recitals. Any facet of entertaining was a joy to her, as long as she was onstage. About the only thing she hadn't done so far was act; there was no time for it, besides school plays, and central Texas didn't offer many outlets for a very young actress. (Killeen, however, was the childhood home of someone else who became something of a television star in the late nineties: Renee O'Connor, who plays Gabrielle on the syndicated *Xena: Warrior Princess*. However, since she was more than ten years older than Love, the two never knew each other.)

So Jennifer Love took advantage of any and every opportunity to shine. Onstage, she had a real magic that went beyond cuteness. When she was nine, she was asked to take part in a dance recital with a number of other girls from central Texas; without thinking twice, she jumped at the chance. All she knew was that it was important; she had no idea why. As always, she went out and gave it her best. She was a good dancer, maybe even the best on the stage, and her performance impressed one man in the audience. He was a talent scout for an organization called the Texas Show Team.

The Show Team was a group of kids who traveled all over the world, entertaining and acting as young ambassadors for the Great State. At the time the scout was putting together a dance troupe, with a specific trip in mind.

"[He] was there and picked me and about twenty ambassadors to go to Russia and be good will ambassadors," Love recalled.

Of course, it wasn't as simple as that; nothing ever is. The trip, which was to include both Russia and Denmark, would last for several weeks at the end of 1988. That meant missing school, and however much Pat Hewitt supported her daughter's ambitions, school had to be the top priority. However, tutors were to be arranged, and it would be the field trip of a lifetime, a chance to see the kind of places other kids could only read about.

It would also be the first time Jennifer was away from her family, so Pat naturally wanted to be sure her little girl was well looked after. The scout assured her that all the girls who went would be treated very well, and be carefully chaperoned. Everything would be fine.

There was still a lot of preparation. Jennifer Love needed a passport, and new clothes had to be bought—Russia and Denmark in winter would be a lot colder than Killeen, Texas.

For Love, it was all one huge adventure, traveling with the other girls, getting to dance before official audiences. It gave her the chance to see that Russians were regular people, too, with regular kids. They might not speak each other's language, but they could smile, and often understand each other without words. To the American kids, it humanized the Russians, characterized just a few years before by President Reagan as "the evil empire." The country's government was taking the first steps away from communism, and politically and economically it was having a difficult time. There was unemployment, many people didn't have much money, the apartments and houses seemed very basic by the standards the American girls were used to at home.

It was the kind of education they could never have got at school. Traveling by train and the creaky, somewhat frightening old planes of the Aeroflot airline, they were able to see just *how* big Russia was, mile after mile after mile of countryside. They drank steaming tea from samovars like the natives, ate the local dishes, and found themselves wishing for McDonald's or Burger King.

Jennifer was never happier than when she was dancing with the others. Prior to the trip, they'd put in a full week of rehearsals, and now it paid off. Onstage they were very professional—after all, they'd been picked because they were the best in the state—able to do their numbers almost without thinking, with excellent coordination. They were cute, lovable, and they danced up a storm.

Denmark was as cold as Russia, but more modern, and had more of what the Texas girls were used to in terms of amenities. They performed in Copenhagen, had a chance to tour the city, and then they were on their way home in time for Christmas 1988.

It had been a remarkable few weeks. Love had seen things she'd never expected to see, met all kinds of people. She brought home presents for Pat and her brother, Todd, who was now in college, and spent hours talking about everything she'd seen, both with her mom and her classmates.

When the Texas Show Team arrived home, there was an official reception for them. As young ambassadors, they'd done very well. Around Texas, the newspapers gave plenty of room to the story; after all, these were local girls who'd made good and performed far, far away. They were a big deal. Love, with her bubbly personality, was one of those interviewed.

But once the wave of publicity was over, things began to settle down to normal. Christmas was coming, there was shopping to be done, a tree to decorate, schoolwork to catch up on. Jennifer settled back into her routine. Even though she was barely home, everything began to seem like a distant memory, like last year's vacation.

Until the phone rang one day. It was someone asking to speak to Pat. The conversation lasted a long time, and when she was done, Pat Hewitt came and sat with her daughter in the living room.

The call had been from a manager in Los Angeles. He'd read about Love in the newspapers and seen her photograph. He thought she might have a future as an actress out in California.

Love was stunned. For years, almost as long as she could remember, she'd dreamed about the idea of being on television or in a movie. She even thought it might happen one day. But she'd never thought it would be like this. This . . . well, it was like something out of a movie. She'd been in show business long enough to know things just didn't happen this way.

What the manager was suggesting, Pat explained, was that Love go to Los Angeles for a month and see if there was any interest. He couldn't guarantee anything, but he wouldn't have called if he didn't believe she had a future. Even if she went, Pat warned, she might just end up coming back home empty-handed.

As soon as the idea was in her head, Jennifer knew it was the right thing to do, the *only* thing to do.

"My mom had this little girl who said, 'I really, really want to do this crazy thing,' " Jennifer said. "I said, 'Please, Mommy. Please, Mommy.' "

With Todd now away at college, just Jennifer and Pat were at home. A month couldn't hurt, Pat reasoned to herself. She knew full well that the odds were stacked against her daughter, and that she most likely would be coming back to Texas, disappointed. But it was her dream, and if she didn't follow it, if she didn't try, she'd never know—and that would be even worse.

There is never room for "what ifs" in life—not even when you're barely ten years old. So Pat agreed—but only for one month, to see how things went.

Love couldn't believe it. She'd hoped her mother would say yes, but a large part of her had been expecting a no. Now she was going to L.A. She really did have a chance to make it.

Chapter Two

The two of them arrived in Los Angeles on Jennifer Love's tenth birthday, February 21, 1989. There was no party, no cake with candles, but this was the best present she could have been given. Even the sight of the city covered in a light brown smoggy haze of pollution as the airplane descended into LAX airport didn't put her off.

She couldn't believe how big the sprawl beneath her was. She'd seen the Dallas–Fort Worth area from the air, but this was way, way bigger, unlike anything she'd ever viewed before. She'd even looked from the window, trying to pick out the "Hollywood" sign, and imagine where it could be below her, but she had no luck.

After collecting their luggage, Pat and Love Hewitt made their way outside. Immediately it seemed so alien from the Texas they'd left behind. It was warm and pleasant, and there were *palm trees* growing everywhere. It was as if they'd landed in Hawaii instead of Los Angeles. Love had seen Russia and Denmark, but she'd never seen anything like *this*.

The trip might have been undertaken for Jennifer's sake, but it was Pat Hewitt who had to attend to all the details. She'd booked the pair of them into a motel, a place to use as their base. There didn't seem to be any sense in renting an apartment when they had no idea if they'd be staying—in fact, when they'd probably be going home again after thirty days. Lots of kids, big and small, came out here to try their luck. Only a very, very few made it.

Once they were booked into the motel, it was time to do some sightseeing, all around Hollywood, the famous places, the places where Love hoped they'd know her one day. Then they would settle down, just the two of them, for a birthday dinner. It had been a long, long, exciting day. And tomorrow might be even longer.

The first thing Love was going to need was representation—a manager and an agent. Los Angeles had no shortage of those. If someone wasn't an agent, they seemed to know someone else who was. After checking, Pat had found out that the manager who'd called her in Killeen was quite legitimate; he wasn't going to scam them or hurt them. He seemed to be the obvious first step. Even before they'd left Texas she'd called him and arranged an appointment for their first full day in California; there was no sense in wasting any time when all you had was a month.

It couldn't have gone any better if it had been scripted. The manager was impressed by Love, her talent, her looks, and her résumé, and Pat was impressed by the manager. She felt confident. He offered to begin sending Love out on auditions, to see if anything happened. Of course, since she was a completely unknown talent in California, she'd just be one of many girls going for a part. But he had a feeling things might happen for her. Even though she'd never really acted, she had poise.

She was also going to need an agent, but luck was with her again. Pat Hewitt's best friend in Killeen had been Lauren Chapin, a former actress who'd played Kitten on the venerable fifties sitcom *Father Knows Best*. Although she'd retired from the business, she still had some contacts, and recommended that Pat and Love talk to a particular agent. They did, and on the strength of Chapin's recommendation and Love's résumé, the girl was signed.

Now the first part was taken care of. Love was going to have her chance, and it would come sooner than she'd imagined—the very next day, in fact. "But before I went on my first audition, my mom and I did our secret handshake and she said 'You have to promise me, no matter what happens, if you don't have a good time, if it's not fun, we go somewhere far, far away.' "

That was the deal they made. And when they walked into the waiting room, full of stage mothers and their precocious daughters, they both wondered for a moment if they were doing the right thing. They were different, from Texas, hicks from the sticks in comparison, not used to this kind of thing. But Pat understood that it was something they were going to have to get used to, even if it was only for thirty days. Her little girl had gone from being someone special, someone who really stood out at home, to being just one of many, all trying their hardest to get a part.

It wasn't even as if this were a *real* acting role. It was just a job in a television commercial. The agent had made it clear, though, that every job, even if it seemed small, was important. Everything Love had done before, the appearances, even the Texas Show Team trip, didn't count for much out here. She was starting from the very beginning, and that meant she had to build up a whole new résumé; commercials were a good way to begin.

It seemed as if the girls barely got a chance to show what they could do; if they didn't impress immediately, that was the end, and it was on to the next audition. At least, here in the center of the television industry, there was no end of opportunities to try again and again and again.

Love watched everything, completely enthralled. Far from hating all this, she was having the time of her life.

She was ten years old, in another city, and trying to become an entertainer. What could be bad about that?

She auditioned, not the least bit nervous once she began to perform. Two minutes and her time was up; it wasn't enough to show what she could *really* do, but it was all she had to impress.

That time she didn't get the part, but the next day and the day after she and Pat went on more auditions, seeing the same faces among the mothers and daughters in the waiting rooms. Within a week, Love did manage to snag her first role. Again, it was just a commercial, for Mattel toys, a Barbie doll ad, but to her it was far more than *just* anything. It was success. She'd come to Hollywood and won. She couldn't have been happier if she'd won the lead in a new, big-budget movie. And not only that, it was *Barbie*—she'd played with Barbie when she was younger, and still had a couple of the dolls in her closet at home. This was *cool*.

Filming was altogether a new experience for her. She'd never been on a soundstage—the building where the filming is done—or a set before. The lights were bright and very hot, there was a constant sense of urgency in the way people talked, but very little actually seemed to get done. Love spent most of her day waiting to work, for the few seconds she'd actually be on camera. Even when her scene was filmed, the director wanted take after take after take, until he was finally satisfied. It was fun, in its own way, watching people, seeing what each one did, but Love also realized that filming was a lot of work. If she was going to start doing it regularly—and she believed in her heart that she would—there were a lot of things she'd have to get used to.

So, within a week, Love Hewitt had gone through her first television job. Pat was quick to point out, though, that one job didn't make her a star. It meant she'd made a start. And they were only in Los Angeles for another three weeks, unless something quite remarkable happened.

Love, needless to say, hoped that something quite remarkable *would* happen. After growing up in Killeen, she thought L.A. seemed exotic, the kind of place she wanted to live. She felt as if she fit in more here, that kids wouldn't make fun of her for putting on plays or wanting to be a performer. In Texas, apart from the local news, you never had the chance to be on television. Here, the opportunities were coming up almost every day. And unlike Killeen, unlike even Dallas, Los Angeles had a place like Hollywood, where you could go to Graumann's Chinese Theater and see the handprints of all the famous movie stars, or somewhere like Sunset, which just seemed to ooze romance, and the roads going off into the Hollywood Hills where all the stars had their houses, where Love might one day have a place of her own.

She was captivated with L.A. But she also knew that, unless she got something more than just one commercial, her mom would insist after a month that they go home. With that one commercial to her credit, she was eager to extend her résumé, and make the absolute most of the time she had left.

Every day there were more auditions, sometimes two or three of them. It was exhausting, maybe more so for Pat than Love, but the girl was going after every opportunity. Commercials weren't what she'd seen herself doing—it didn't seem like acting, it didn't really seem like anything—but if that was the best way into show business, that was the path she'd take. She landed two more parts, and received callbacks for a couple of others.

To Love, it felt as if she were really on her way. Three parts in a month was good going; she'd learned that much from talking to the other girls at auditions.

And it had been great to have time off from school to follow this dream. But as the month drew to a close, she knew the decision was going to be her mom's. What Pat Hewitt decided was what had to happen.

Pat already knew what her daughter wanted—to stay in Los Angeles and keep working. To be fair, she'd worked really hard, and she'd been very successful. She'd done more in a month than a lot of the girls managed in a year—the other mothers had told her that. Love had drive, ambition, and a whole lot of talent.

But this month was something different. No school, living in a motel. Pat couldn't help wondering how Love would feel if they lived here and she was going to school every day, then trying to go to auditions afterward, juggling schedules to try and film this or that, whatever parts she managed to get. There was no doubt she had *something* that set her apart, but was it enough to really succeed? She was like all parents—she didn't want to see her girl's dreams crushed. In Texas she was a big fish in a little pond—an even bigger fish now that she had some television credits. Out here she was still very much just one of the crowd.

It was a difficult decision to make, and the two of them talked about it for a long time. Pat understood, probably much more than Love, that entertaining was what the girl had been born to do. Wherever it had come from, it was a part of her, and there could be no denying it, nor the fact that she was very good at it. A speech pathologist could practice anywhere. Whether in Texas or California, there was no shortage of clients. But an actress, singer, and dancer had to be where the work was. Finally, they decided: Los Angeles would be their new home.

No one ever said moving was easy. Pat had to give notice at work, sell the house in Killeen. All the family possessions had to be sorted through, many discarded and the rest packed. They needed to rent an apartment in Los Angeles—and decide where they wanted to live in the City of Angels—arrange to have everything moved... a never-ending series of problems. For Pat, even more than Love, Texas was home; she'd be leaving her foundations. And even though Todd was in college now, a freshman, living away from home, that didn't make the knowledge that his mom and sister were moving to the West Coast any easier.

Pat coped with it all. To Love it all seemed like a big adventure. She'd always felt different from the other kids at school. Now she was going to a place where she'd have more in common with people, where her goals wouldn't seem so weird, where she'd have the chance to do everything she wanted.

Things moved remarkably quickly, and it was just a very few months before Pat and Love Hewitt were unpacking boxes in their new apartment in Burbank. They'd chosen the area because of its closeness to most of the television studios. That, hopefully, was where Love would be auditioning and working—it was where they'd spent a lot of their time on their earlier trip.

There was still plenty to sort out. They'd moved for Love's career, but she was still only ten years old, which meant she'd be spending five days a week in school. Performing was fine, but a good education came first. Auditions and everything else would have to fit around that.

And that was the way it was. Love felt strange at school at first, the way a new kid always does, particularly one with a different accent—she still had her Texas twang then—but she quickly settled into the rhythm, made some new friends, and began to adapt.

Of course, she continued to go to auditions. Her agent set them up, and Love seemed to have a remarkable success rate. There were more Barbie commercials, an ad for Chex cereal, and others. What she really wanted, though, was to be in a series, to be someone like Soleil Moon Frye on *Punky Brewster*, or even, sometime, Molly Ringwald in those John Hughes teen movies that had been so popular during the eighties, and which Love had seen and kept on video.

A TV series, though, was altogether different from an ad. In an ad you were just onscreen for a few seconds. A series went on week after week; it would be a lot of work. As an actress, Love definitely wasn't ready for a drama or a sitcom. She still had a long ways to go.

However, there were no doubts about her ability to sing and dance, and she could project well onscreen—something that helped make her very popular and brought more work. If there was a job in a series where she could utilize those talents, then there might really be something...

But there was one series that would suit Love perfectly: the Disney Channel's *Kids Incorporated*. It had been on the air for six years and featured music, singing, dancing, and skits, all performed by the cast—who were all kids.

The show was very professional, and caught the audience it was aiming for—other kids. If Love could find something like that, then she knew she could be successful at it.

The only problem was that there was nothing else quite like it on television. Shows for kids that actually employed kids were very few and far between. It wasn't that she was without work, since work on commercials kept coming, but she wanted to be able to stretch herself, to be seen as a real person.

That was why, when her agent called to say there was a spot opening up on *Kids Incorporated*, Love was thrilled. This was her chance to show everyone what she could really do. She was already sharp from all her auditions, but she immediately began rehearsing more, in preparation for the upcoming audition.

She knew there'd be plenty of competition, but neither she nor her mother was prepared for the crowd they encountered when they arrived. It was as if every girl in Los Angeles had come to try out.

"I auditioned with eleven hundred other girls for the part," Love recalled. Obviously she was as impressive as she'd hoped, because she was called back and called back as the producers whittled down the numbers.

She was auditioning to play a girl called Robin. The role would offer incredible exposure for whoever won it. Not only would it mean regular work on the show, but there would undoubtedly be plenty of other opportunities—commercials, appearances. It would look great on her résumé, which was growing every single month. Love was quickly becoming a seasoned performer, used to the way that things happened.

She was still able to become excited about everything that was happening, though. It was all still an adventure, even the auditions, still a joy, and a total thrill whenever she got good news.

All the commercials paled next to this, however. With each callback, Love kept making the cut, and becoming more and more tense as she knew her chance of being Robin was increasing. Pat didn't want her to get her hopes too high—anything could happen, and she didn't want her girl despondent—but she too thought Love had a great chance.

"They finally narrowed it down to two [of us]," Love said, "and I originally didn't get the part, and then [I] was called two weeks later, and the girl that had originally got it couldn't do it, so I got to do it."

First she had to go through the lows—coming so close, *so* close, but not making it. Then, after she'd resigned herself to the loss, the second chance came, and there was no way she was going to turn it down.

Whatever happened to the other girl couldn't have worked out better for Love. All of a sudden she found herself with a very busy schedule. Not only was she going to school, but there were also rehearsals with the rest of the cast, then the tapings of the episodes. She could have done what many kids in show business did, and had a tutor on the set, but Pat wanted her to have a normal life, too, to know kids who just led regular lives.

One thing that had worried Love was that, when she'd seen *Kids Incorporated*, the cast always looked as if they were playing instruments during their songs, and she didn't play any instrument, let alone the keyboard that Robin was supposed to play. So it was a relief to learn that although she'd be doing her own singing—which came easily to her—"we were fake-playing the instruments."

As one of six members of the cast, Love got plenty of screen time, and her first real chance to act, during the show's skits and sketches. The demands on her were high, but she was more than up to the challenge, the equal of the more experienced cast members.

Once she'd settled in, Love felt really at home on the show. She'd been nervous at first, she was the new kid on the block, but the others welcomed her. It proved to be the ideal first experience for a young actress.

"It was my first job," she'd recall later, "and it was kind of like a dream come true because I loved to sing, loved to dance, and loved hanging out with people my own age, so it was a lot of fun."

However, it wasn't the only fun in her life. Love might have been busy, but once she was used to the routine, she couldn't resist going after other opportunities. The first of those was auditioning for a print ad campaign for L.A. Gear sports shoes and clothing.

With more confidence, and her ability growing every day, Love found herself among the finalists, and was soon selected. What she didn't know at the time was that she'd be featured with the main spokesman for L.A. Gear—none other than the music superstar of the eighties, Michael Jackson!

That was another coup for a girl who was still only ten years old, and who'd only come to Los Angeles a few months before.

Kids Incorporated had finished filming for the season by the time the campaign began, which left Love free to take part in phase two—she was part of a group who were set to tour under the L.A. Gear banner, putting on performances, singing and dancing. In other words, exactly the things she did very well anyway!

It was a great international opportunity, a chance to literally travel the world, going around the U.S., Asia, and Europe. Of course, just the year before she'd been to Russia and Denmark, but this would take her much farther.

The only problem was that the school year wasn't yet over. Love still had to complete her grade. It was arranged that tutors would accompany the kids, making sure they kept up with their schooling. Pat sat down and negotiated with the school principal, who reluctantly agreed to let Love go, on one condition: that she send letters to her class.

Mixing a "regular" life with being an entertainer had seemed like a good idea to Pat, a way of keeping her daughter grounded. But the school's attitude made her wonder if she'd made the right decision. Instead of being the popular girl because she was doing so much, Love's classmates, and her teachers, tended to look at her as "the freak that wanted to act and not play Nintendo. I was looked at as very off-the-wall, even by my teachers. I never really fit in." It was like Killeen all over again, not at all what she'd hoped or expected.

She felt much happier on the set, or on the road, traveling from one big city to another, from one country to the next, taking her lessons in short bursts, writing her letters to her school and knowing that all the girls probably wanted to be her, deep down.

If the schedule when she was filming *Kids Incorporated* had been tiring, this was grueling. As well as traveling, trying to sightsee and buy presents, there was school, and four thirty-minute performances every day. She had barely enough time to sleep!

Of course, Michael Jackson wasn't part of the touring ensemble; he had much bigger fish to fry. But that was hardly a disappointment to Love. In fact, it helped her. The people who came to see the performers could focus on her and the others. If Jackson had been there, no one would have even noticed her. As it was, she was at the center of attention.

By the time she arrived back in Los Angeles, Love was tired. The last few weeks had been busy. The last few *months* had been busy. But there was no time to relax, to kick back and enjoy the summer by hanging out the way other girls her age were doing. Once she'd had a few days to get over her jet lag, Love was due back on the set of *Kids Incorporated*, to play Robin for another season.

It meant more work, no real time for herself or to just be a kid, but that was what she'd wanted. She'd convinced her mom to come out to L.A. so she could try to make it, and now that everything was happening for her she wasn't going to let anything go. Everything she did helped everything else. Each experience was good, even the bad ones; they all added to her professionalism, and by now Love Hewitt was nothing if not professional.

Chapter Three

By her second season on *Kids Incorporated,* Love was a fully integrated member of the cast, used to the rigors of rehearsal and filming, learning the new dances and songs every week. She continued in her regular school; it might not be the perfect solution, but it did let her know that life didn't completely revolve around show business.

She also took time to audition and win more commercials, a career that was proving very good for her. A Disney Channel show on her résumé and a growing line of ad credits certainly helped things along, but it was her talent and presence on a stage that really caused her to be noticed by the directors.

Love had become something of a regular in commercials for Barbie, and would actually go on to make more than twenty of them for the same product. But that wasn't her only association with the famous doll. Early in 1991 a casting call went out—there was going to be a Barbie video. This was at the height of the workout video phase, when it seemed as if every celebrity of any note was making his or her own workout video, following the astonishing success of those by Jane Fonda.

Dance! Workout With Barbie appealed to a different market. The others were all targeted at adults, many of whom needed to shed a few pounds, or just stay in shape. This was aimed directly at girls. It was sad, but true, that Americans—young and old—were becoming couch potatoes. Kids weren't outside, running and playing the way they once had. Instead, cable TV and video games were keeping them inside. They weren't exercising as much. So anything that helped them get up and moving had to be a good thing.

The format would be an animated Barbie leading nine girls through a workout, which meant that nine girls had to be selected from the hundreds who applied for the roles.

Love was one of those girls, although her experience, both on *Kids Incorporated* and in the Barbie commercials, gave her a definite head start over most of the applicants. As was the case with the Disney show, the producers kept calling girls back for more auditions, and Love's name stayed on the list, until she made the final cut and was signed for the video!

Maybe it didn't have the glamour of a feature film, or even the prestige of a television series, but it was work, it was something that would be seen by many thousands of kids, and above all, it was *fun*! That was still the important thing. Pat Hewitt kept telling her daughter that if acting and performing ever stopped being fun, she should just quit. There were plenty of other things in life, and lots of other careers to pursue.

But Love couldn't imagine doing anything else. This was what she lived for, being in front of an audience or a camera and shining.

And making the video *was* a lot of fun. It was essentially dancing, something she'd been doing for years now, following all the choreography. She'd done a lot of things like this before, but it was the first time she'd worked with an animated figure, although Barbie herself wouldn't be added until the whole thing was complete.

Dancing wasn't the only contribution Love made to *Dance! Workout With Barbie*. To dance you needed music, in particular, *songs*. All the material for the video was original, but someone, a kid, was needed to perform it. That was where Love came to the forefront again. By now she was used to singing, to recording a performance and a song, so she was a natural choice to sing all the songs on the video. The star on the box might have been Barbie, but it was Love Hewitt whom everyone kept seeing and hearing.

On top of the weekly show and school, the video was a strain, but more than worthwhile. Love was having the time of her life, doing everything. And she still managed to keep her grades high, which was perhaps the biggest feat of all.

Guests would sometimes appear on *Kids Incorporated*, and during Love's second season on the show, there was one she'd end up encountering again a few years later.

Scott Wolf was hardly a star when he appeared on the program. He'd done a couple of commercials and had a very brief role in the sitcom *Saved by the Bell*, where he played a waiter. *Kids Incorporated* was actually his biggest role so far—in more ways than one, since he played a double role, as twins Billy and Bobby, in a sketch with series regular Eric (Eric Balfour). With a very young face and small build, Scott, who was actually twenty-three years old at the time—more than a decade older than Love—looked very convincing as a teenager.

Of course, neither Love nor Scott could have any idea that their paths would cross again, and so closely, in just a few short years.

Love Hewitt was a real success story. Everything she'd dreamed of doing had come true. But even she couldn't get every role she went after. As with every career, there would be setbacks.

"When I was eleven, I lost a movie and it tore me to pieces," she recalled. "I was close to telling my mom to call the airlines and let's go home to Texas. But then I talked to my acting coach for three hours and he told me, 'You have such a drive and such a love for what you do. Do you have any idea how miserable you will be if you don't do this?' The next day I was booked in another job and I got over it."

He was right, and he offered her the perfect advice. If she was going to act, she also had to learn to cope with some rejection; it came with the territory, and the sooner she learned to accept that it was nothing personal, the better. It was a lesson she would take to heart, understanding eventually that she'd need her drive to keep herself going.

"I don't think you can be an actress without ambition," she'd muse. "So much of the acting world is about rejection, so without that drive I don't think I'd be able to take it."

For now, it wasn't as if she didn't have enough to keep her busy. But Love wanted new challenges, and being in a movie, a *real* movie, would have been wonderful.

It would all happen in time, Pat Hewitt assured her. For now, though, there was the show, and plenty of commercials, from more Barbie to one that Love would recall as particularly embarrassing.

"I did this commercial where I was rollerblading holding these loaves of bread, and then I was pretending to be swimming, still holding the bread . . ."

But she didn't write them, she just acted, and that was what they paid her to do.

The hours of dancing lessons and time spent working with the acting coach were all paying off in a very big way. At least, they were professionally. At school people continued to give her a hard time.

"My teachers said that I was ruining my life because I was acting, and that I was going to end up stupid because I wasn't going to have a good education. Yet,

I had traveled the world, I had social skills, and I was a straight-A student."

What more could they want from her? She was the odd one out, the girl who didn't have time for the regular pleasures of hanging out because she had other dreams she was pursuing. And it was true that she had very little free time. But she was doing everything her teachers requested, and doing it better than most of the kids in the class.

It all meant that Love was much happier on the set than anywhere else, except at home with her mom. Around other people who thought the way she did, who were professionals like herself, she could really come alive. She didn't hate learning, and her problems at school were caused by other people. However, it formed a gulf in her life, as if there were two Love Hewitts, one who had to try and be "normal" in an attempt to fit in, and the other who could just be herself.

Professionally, however, things were moving ahead at a good pace. As a singer she'd come a long way from the three-year-old who'd crooned "Help Me Make It Through the Night" in a Texas supper club, or even from the girl singing Whitney Houston in a cleaned-out pig barn. It was obvious that, at twelve, her voice had developed into a very supple and very good instrument, enough to make her the standout vocalist on *Kids Incorporated*.

These days, although singing was an important part of her life, Love was thinking of herself more as an actress. That was what she wanted to do. So it came as a total shock when her next big break came from music.

Her work on *Dance! Workout With Barbie* and on *Kids Incorporated* had brought her some attention in, of all places, Japan. She was approached about the possibility of making a record for release there.

It was an idea that had never occurred to her before. Of course, she bought records, and she had her own favorites among bands and singers, but she'd never really thought that she might end up among them. Singing was just something she did, something she loved, a part of her. However, the Japanese record label, Medlac Records, seemed to think it was a good idea, and Love had absolutely nothing to lose by doing it. The contract specified that it would be released only in Japan, so if it turned out to be really horrible, no one she knew would ever hear it. And if it was great, maybe it would find release in America.

The album was a mix of pop music and ballads, including the lovely "Love (What's It Gonna Take?)." The dance tracks were very upbeat, and one of them, "Dancing Queen," was actually issued as a single.

"It did really well," Love remembered. "I had the number one dance song on the [Japanese] charts for four weeks." It did so well, in fact, that the single was also issued in England, Germany, Switzerland, and Austria.

The album, entitled *Love Songs,* was issued in 1992, just as Love became a teenager. There were eleven tracks in all, all well suited to a girl of her age, and in some ways not too dissimilar from the records Alanis Morrissette made as a young girl in Canada, where she was a star.

The record never did appear in the United States, for which an older and wiser Jennifer Love Hewitt is now very grateful.

"I was only twelve years old when I did that and it's kind of embarrassing because I was so little!"

In fact, there was little to be embarrassed about. While the idea of a twelve-year-old going into a recording studio seemed like a bit of a novelty, Love really could sing, and put every bit of herself into her performances. And having a number one dance song wasn't at all that shabby. The hit and the record itself were more things to go on her résumé, to demonstrate her versatility. More than that, they showed she could succeed at something else.

The standout track on *Love Songs,* however, was "Please Save Us the World," which she recorded with the rest of the group from *Kids Incorporated.*

As the title implied, it was a song about ecology and conservation, as well as a plea to stop war. Not only did the group perform it on the show, but during 1992 they were also guests on the United Cerebral Palsy telethon and sang it there, too. Over the course of the year it became something of an anthem for them, and they went so far as to make a music video of it, featuring not only the cast, but a whole host of other young celebrities.

In fact, the song seemed to take on a life of its own. The Earth Summit, a gathering to discuss environmental issues, in Rio de Janeiro, Brazil, also took place in 1992, and "Please Save Us the World" was considered so great that it was named the official song of the summit, and Love was appointed as America's youth ambassador to the gathering in Rio—a singular honor. The ambassadorship had come about because of her acting and her singing, but in the end it had nothing to do with that.

By now her career was really starting to sizzle. The summer before, after completing her second season on *Kids Incorporated,* she auditioned for, and won, her first movie role, in a film that appeared during the summer of 1992.

It's true that Love won't be remembered for the role of Andrea in *Munchie.* The movie, directed by Jim Wynorski, was a sequel to 1987's *Munchies,* which had itself been something of a spoof or rip-off (depending on your point of view) of 1984's *Gremlins* (which had itself spawned a sequel in 1990). *Munchie* was a comedy, although not a particularly funny one. The big name star was Loni Anderson, who'd come to prominence in the TV sitcom *WKRP in Cincinnati,* then as

Burt Reynolds's wife. The lead, though, was Jamie McEnnan, who played Gage Dobson. In a mine shaft, he discovered the Munchie (whose voice was provided by Dom DeLuise), an ancient alien creature with strange powers. The Munchie turned out to be friendly, and able to help Gage, at least to an extent. His powers kept the school bullies at bay, and helped Gage get Andrea, the girl of his dreams. But even an alien couldn't stop him from getting in trouble at school or with his mom. Still, all ended well, and everyone lived happily ever after.

Made on a tiny budget, *Munchie* was never expected to do particularly well at the box office. It was the type of movie that was made for a market that hardly existed any more: the drive-in theater. People wouldn't deliberately spend money on such a film, and sit in a movie theater to watch it.

It did mean, though, that Love now had a movie on her résumé. She was really beginning to branch out, to fulfill the potential she'd shown over the last couple of years.

She was growing, both as a girl and as a performer, and she was eager to seek new challenges and opportunities. In the last twelve months she'd done so much—a movie, an album, being appointed youth ambassador—and she was ready to take on even more.

During the spring of 1992, she'd filmed her first television drama, a pilot for a series called *Running Wilde,* which starred Pierce Brosnan, still riding high from his *Remington Steele* series. He played a reporter for an automobile magazine, and Love was his daughter. The show was made for NBC with the hope that it would become the basis for a series. Unfortunately, the network didn't care for the idea. The series wasn't picked up, and the pilot show was never screened on television.

It was a setback for Love, but only a minor one. For every step back she seemed to be taking three forward. Once the season for *Kids Incorporated* was over, she signed to make another film, and also found herself auditioning for another television series, this time for the upstart FOX network, one that was more willing to take chances.

This time the pilot *was* picked up, which meant that Love was going to be a part of the cast, and would be spending the next few months on the set.

In turn, that meant she needed to make quite a few changes in her life. It was hard, because she'd become friends with all the others on the show, but Love had to say goodbye to her role of Robin on *Kids Incorporated*. After three seasons she still loved the show and everyone she worked with, but she needed something fresh, and there was simply no way she could juggle her schedule to do both *Kids Incorporated* and the new series.

It was a big leap into the unknown, but exactly what she needed to do for her career. Everything has a beginning and an end, and Love's time as Robin had come to an end. She'd explored all she could with the character, fun as it had been. The show had brought her a long way, and helped make her into a true professional.

The other big change was much easier to make. As a minor, the amount of time she could work on the set each day was strictly regulated. Making a series, though, was very time-consuming. Love had to be there, and be available, from Monday to Friday every week. So it was impossible to keep attending the regular school she'd be going to, where'd she'd been so unhappy. She was going to have a tutor on the set, and she'd do her lessons between takes.

Pat had known it would happen eventually, if Love continued as she had been, but she'd tried to delay it as long as possible. Now there was no chance of putting it off any longer. Love was a success, and needed to do it this way now. Love Hewitt wouldn't be going back to school.

Chapter Four

Canadian actor Matt Frewer had made his name in one of the eighties' most unusual series, *Max Headroom,* playing the title character, who was nothing more than a computer-generated face on a screen. Although the character became something of a cult figure (featured in a song and video by the band Art of Noise), the series itself didn't do so well; most people just didn't "get it." After less than a season on the air, in 1987, it was canceled due to low ratings.

Frewer himself appeared from time to time in other shows, but was never quite able to shake the Max Headroom tag. He was hoping that a gap of five years might make all the difference when he signed to star in the new FOX series, *Shaky Ground.*

In an era when "downsizing" had become a word everyone knew too well, with workers who assumed they had jobs for life suddenly finding themselves unemployed, others having hours cut back and benefits removed, the financial problems of a white-collar worker were something a lot of Americans could relate to. All of a sudden, corporate America was discovering that it had far too many employees, that its payrolls were too high, and that the burden of work could be focused on a much tighter group. It was a time when people all over the country feared for their jobs on a daily basis. Men who had been climbing the ladder to success for years, who made very good money, found themselves without jobs, trying vainly to get new positions as, all around them, their neighbors and friends also suddenly found themselves out of work.

Downsizing became the watchword of business, and it was applied ruthlessly—often overzealously, as time would prove. But it meant that those who were employed became very careful, cutting back on their spending, trying to quickly accumulate a nest egg of money just in case they were the next ones to go.

That was the cultural backdrop of *Shaky Ground*. Like so many series, and like life itself, it would be a mix of comedy and drama—but mostly comedy. Frewer was picked to play Bob Moody, a fairly typical white-collar worker whose income never seemed to stretch quite far enough, what with his mortgage, car payment, and a family to support. On top of that, however hard he worked, and whatever ideas he came up with, Moody could never seem to get ahead at work; in fact, the danger of the job being yanked out from under him was a constant threat. Whatever happened, Bob Moody couldn't win.

Of course, a man like that had to have a sassy daughter, and that was where Love came into the picture. She auditioned and won the role of Bernadette, a smart, cute girl just starting her teens (as Love was herself).

After the pilot of *Running Wilde* had failed to make the cut, Love was understandably worried about this new project. But it wasn't necessary. FOX, still barely three years old, needed shows to be able to expand and compete as a network. *Shaky Ground* had the green light.

For Love, working on a series like this was real freedom. She was on the set every weekday, happy to work with her tutor when she wasn't filming or rehearsing. Away from all the distractions of the other kids in class, and the way they and the teachers had picked on her, she was able to focus completely on her lessons, even if they came in short spurts. And the chance to really act spurred her on professionally. Frewer was a fine actor, and keeping up with him demanded a great deal from her.

Although she'd never had formal acting lessons, Love had worked with an acting coach periodically, mostly to prepare for her auditions, and now she began to realize just how much she'd learned from him. There were techniques and tips she'd picked up that proved to be very handy.

The work was grueling, and the pressure was intense. Not only did they have to keep every episode on budget and on schedule, but the child labor laws meant that Love could only be on the set for a limited number of hours each day, so her scenes had to be carefully planned, and executed right the first time. She couldn't be a little prima donna; instead, she had to rely on the professionalism she'd built up over recent years.

It was exhausting, but she enjoyed every second, and when *Shaky Ground* aired for the first time, in the fall of 1992, she felt a great deal of pride at 7 P.M. that Sunday night.

The show's biggest problem was its time slot. It had wide appeal, and it was a good show, but anything that went against *60 Minutes* was fighting a losing battle from the beginning. The CBS news show had killed all its competition for many years, even established shows with fairly solid fan bases. For a new show, starring people who were far from household names, it was almost the kiss of death.

And that's exactly what it proved to be. Right from the beginning, *Shaky Ground* did poorly in the ratings. FOX didn't move it to another time slot to try and give it a chance to grow. Instead, *Shaky Ground* stayed where it was, to wither and die like the majority of shows tried on television. It simply never had the opportunity to find its audience. After a total of seventeen episodes, *Shaky Ground* was canceled.

Up to now, Love hadn't been very successful when it came to television series. However, she had more strings to her bow than just that. After *Munchie*, her film career had definitely begun to take off. Even before she began work on *Shaky Ground*, she finished a second film, which was released late in 1993.

Little Miss Millions was financed by Concorde Pictures, and it was an unabashedly sentimental holiday film, aimed squarely at the Christmas market. It also offered Love her first major big-screen role, with plenty of time for her face to be seen in the theaters. While she was hardly the biggest name in the film (that belonged to Howard Hesseman, who'd starred in the TV sitcom *WKRP in Cincinnati;* by coincidence, his colleague from that show, Loni Anderson, had been in Love's previous film), she was very definitely the center of attention.

Love played Heather Lofton, a nine-year-old girl who lived with her rather wicked stepmother. What made Heather different was the fact that she was worth literally millions of dollars, money she'd inherited from her late father. It was money that the stepmother wanted for herself, and she treated Heather badly—so badly that the girl ran away.

A bounty hunter, Nick Frost (Howard Hesseman), was hired to find her. His fee, on bringing her home, was to be a very cool half a million dollars.

He did find Heather, which proved not to be too difficult, and returned the reluctant girl to her stepmother, fully expecting to be paid. She refused to hand over his money, though, and began claiming that it was Frost who'd kidnapped the girl, and had tried to ransom her back. The Feds were on Frost's trail.

Naturally, someone from an established family was going to be believed before a down-at-heel bounty hunter, and Frost found himself in a lot of trouble. The only person who could really help him was the one who knew the truth, Heather herself.

They formed an uneasy alliance against both the stepmother and the Feds who were trying to track Frost down. What Heather wanted was to be reunited with her real mother, whom she was sure still loved her for herself rather than for the fortune she possessed. If Frost could help her find her mom, she'd help him clear his name.

It wasn't easy; they could both end up in serious trouble. But neither had much of a choice. They were battling against the odds, but if they won, they'd both be happy, and more to the point, the stepmother would end up with nothing except a lot of grief.

Naturally, there was a happy ending. Heather found her real mother, who was overjoyed to have her daughter back again, and Nick's name was cleared, with the stepmother shown up for the witch that she really was beneath her society manners. Just in time for Christmas, all the good guys got something lovely.

It wasn't meant to be high art or deep drama. Who wanted that in a Christmas movie? It was simply good family entertainment, where the good guys were good, and the bad guys were really bad.

Heather Lofton was by far the biggest role of Love's career, bigger than either of her series. And she took to the part like a duck to water.

It wasn't easy playing someone so much younger than herself. While Heather was supposed to be nine, Love was, in fact, thirteen when the filming took place. But she was physically small for her age, not yet at her full five feet three inches, which definitely helped. The most important thing, though, was her talent, which was really beginning to blossom. *Shaky Ground* hadn't given her much of a chance to act, and neither had *Munchie*, while *Kids Incorporated* had required next to nothing in the way of acting skill from her. This was the first real test of what she could do and where she might go in the future, and she passed it with flying colors.

Heather Lofton was a girl wise beyond her young years (possibly one of the reasons that someone a little older was selected to play her), and certainly no fool about what was going on in her family, particularly concerning her stepmother. Love was able to put that across very well, with frank good humor and an impeccable sense of timing.

The movie wasn't a huge Christmas breakout hit, but *Little Miss Millions* (or *Little Miss Zillions*, as it was also known as a working title) didn't totally bomb. It achieved enough popularity to become something of a staple on television during the holiday season, where it's often screened under the title *Home for Christmas* (but shouldn't be confused with another movie of that name, starring Mickey Rooney).

All in all, Love Hewitt had managed to put together a very impressive résumé in the four years she'd spent in Los Angeles. Many actresses twice her age would have been hard-pressed to have achieved as much in the same time. Series, films, plenty of commercials . . . it truly seemed as if moving to California had been the right thing to do. She was sure of that even when she experienced those moments of frustration or disappointment after losing the role she'd auditioned for.

The problem, however, was that she couldn't just rely on a résumé. Love had to keep proving herself, had to keep growing and pushing for new parts, new roles in which she could challenge herself and prove herself, and in the process become better known. A series that lasted and did well in the ratings would have been ideal, or a movie that did well at the box office; anything that meant people recognized the name Love Hewitt.

Or possibly not Love Hewitt. Although she'd used that name all her life, it wasn't her full name. But as she was growing, the time had come to take on a slightly different identity, to reclaim her full name for professional purposes.

"Since I was a kid everyone's always called me Love," she explained, "and for a long time I just didn't put [Jennifer] on the beginning of my name because I just didn't think about it."

When she did stop to think about it, the full name seemed much better for someone who was rapidly becoming a young woman. It definitely had a more grown-up sound; it was a lot less cute and more serious.

She used it for the first time in the credits for her next movie. In May of 1993 the newly renamed Jennifer "Love" Hewitt was picked to join the cast of *Sister Act 2: Back in the Habit*.

The first *Sister Act* movie had been a huge success for the Disney studio, pulling in almost $140 million during 1992, in spite of bad reviews, and it had made a true star of its lead, Whoopi Goldberg. Although there were rumors of strife between the star and the studio, Goldberg allowed herself to be tempted back for the sequel by a salary that was reportedly between $6.5 and $7.5 million, which made her the highest-paid actress in Hollywood at the time; Disney obviously believed they could re-create the magic of the original film and make another financial killing.

There were, however, a number of problems. While many of the cast from the first film reprised their roles, the director, Emile Ardolino, was ill and unable to work. He was replaced by Bill Duke, who'd directed *A Rage in Harlem* and *Deep Cover*. And even as production got under way, revisions were being made to the script.

Jennifer Love played Margaret, one of the girls at St. Francis High, where Whoopi's character Sister Mary Clarence—known away from the convent as Deloris Van Cartier—had been sent to try and boost the school's finances to keep it open. Among Jennifer's classmates in the film was a girl called Alex Martin, who was, in fact, Goldberg's daughter, Alexandrea.

Jennifer had been picked not merely because she could act, but also because she could sing and dance, a necessity in a film that Goldberg described as "Deloris is back. The nuns are back. We got some priests. We got some intense kids. It's an all-singing, all-dancing, all-acting kind of thing."

The singing, dancing, and acting were all second nature to Jennifer by now, and she was more than able to participate in the musical numbers that helped propel the film.

St. Francis High was supposed to be an inner-city school, with all the stereotypical problems: the kids were tough, and didn't want to learn, the teachers walked in fear of being attacked. Part of the movie's problem was that it took this element too seriously, with sections that seemed like they'd been taken from the 1955 drama *The Blackboard Jungle,* then randomly mixed with scenes from *Fame* and *Welcome Back, Kotter.* It was quickly apparent that, for all the script revisions, plenty of work still needed to be done.

That showed when the movie appeared, relatively quickly, late in 1993, less than six months after shooting had wrapped. While the original had been joyous and funny, *Sister Act 2: Back in the Habit* lacked both those qualities, as the critics rapidly noticed. In the *New York Times*, Caryn James wrote that "the sequel suffers from a lame, saccharine premise and a fatally earnest manner," while *Newsday* felt that it "decided to accentuate the negative and eliminate the positive from *Sister Act . . . Sister Act* [2] is far too silly a concept to support heavy subplots, and the efforts are painfully protracted."

It was a problem common to so many sequels that were made simply to cash in on the popularity of the original. The first movie might have been hilarious and wonderful, but coming up with another equally good storyline for the same characters could prove difficult, or, in this case, impossible. Disney had gone into the project with high hopes for a money-making machine, but when the film only managed to gross slightly under $57 million (which was less than half of the original), they realized that all good things had to come to an end.

For Jennifer Love Hewitt, *Sister Act 2: Back in the Habit* had been little more than a brief experience. Her character, Margaret, was little more than one of the crowd of singing and dancing kids in the movie, and there was little opportunity for her to demonstrate her rapidly developing acting skills. She did get to work around two strong actors, Goldberg and Maggie Smith (whose résumé included *The Prime of Miss Jean Brodie* and *A Room with a View*), but it was impossible for her to feel singled out. And in what turned out to be a very quick shoot, there was little feeling of camaraderie among the cast; Jennifer never really got to *know* anybody.

It was another credit to add to the ever-expanding list, but while the movie was quite high-profile, with plenty of advertising, very few people even noticed her. In some ways that was a relief, but in others it meant that she still wasn't getting the big break that all actresses need to push through to the next level. Jennifer Love Hewitt was happy to work hard, but it was impossible not to feel that she was banging her head against a brick wall. The pilots she was in didn't get picked up, or if they did, the series barely had a chance to get off the ground before being canceled. Her movies didn't attract huge audiences—some of them barely even got reviewed. She was still in search of that one thing that would really get her noticed, and maybe the next project would be it, or the one after that. She had to keep looking, to find it.

Jennifer Love had reached the point where it wasn't

going to be possible for her to play any more nine-year-olds, however. Physical maturity had started quite early for her, as her breasts began to appear when she was twelve.

"I woke up one day and I thought, 'T-shirts will never be the same for me.' It took me a very long time to get used to. For the first two or three years I wore huge sweaters and didn't even want to be a part of what was going on with me."

In that regard, she dressed much like Sarah Reeves in her early days on *Party of Five,* one of many areas where the character and the real person would be very similar. Eventually, Love did come to terms with her body (much as it would seem that Sarah did, judging by the change in her wardrobe).

"And then I just accepted them as a great accessory to every outfit. I was like, 'Who needs a necklace when you have those?' "

The changes meant that she could undertake teenage roles, roles that were more complex, and definitely more of an acting challenge. Jennifer was still—and remains—very much the good girl, without a rebellious bone in her body, possibly because she's been able to express herself in so many roles that have called for different amounts of angst.

But that elusive great series, where she could make her mark, remained out of her grasp. Until she was asked to audition for a new show. It was being developed by Steven Bochco, the man behind *Hill Street Blues* and many other successful television dramas, and it would be called *Byrds of Paradise*.

Bochco's success had made him a real power in television. His ideas, and his scripts, were developed in large part because he seemed to have the magic touch, and all the networks wanted to work with someone like that. So *Byrds of Paradise* had been picked up by ABC.

This was very definitely a family show, revolving

around the Byrd family, with Timothy Busfield starring as Sam Byrd. He played a man who'd been a professor of ethics at Yale, but quit his job after his wife was killed in a robbery. Along with his children, he moved to the Hawaiian island of Oahu, and took a job as the principal of a small school. Apart from the scenic location (which had worked very well for *Hawaii Five-0*), the show's appeal would revolve around the family's dynamics, with the kids growing, and adjusting both to life without their mother and a completely new culture.

Jennifer Love Hewitt won the role of Franny Byrd, and for the first time she was playing someone quite different from herself.

"She was full of teen angst, smoking, yelling at people, driving her dad's car off a cliff. I am not like that."

At fifteen, Franny Byrd was going through a lot of changes. She resented being moved to a place far from what she considered home. She was going through all the changes that fifteen-year-olds go through. And she was missing her mom, having to deal with the fact that she'd never see her again. For Jennifer, who was beginning to feel the pressures of being a teenager, the role was especially cathartic.

"It was at a time in my life when everything was very confusing," she said, "and I found myself frustrated a lot. I got to live out my frustration in [Franny] every single day. So, I'd say playing those parts made me a better teenager."

The show, which was actually filmed on location on Oahu, premiered on ABC in March 1994, just after Jennifer Love had turned fifteen. Filming there was fun, even if, like her character, she found herself uprooted from everything familiar, although Pat Hewitt did travel with her. There was little time for her to experience culture shock. When she wasn't working on the set, she was being tutored. And most of her free time was spent sleeping.

Not all of it, though. She did get to do something she'd never thought of at all—attend a school prom. Actor Kirk Nakama, who was an extra on the show, was preparing for his senior prom, but didn't have a date. He decided that Jennifer would be the perfect person to accompany him.

"He found out that I was from Texas and sent me a dozen yellow roses and asked me to be his date for the prom."

With an invitation like that, how could she refuse? It was a completely new and novel experience for her, doing something most normal teenagers did, mingling with other kids around her own age.

But *Byrds of Paradise* seemed to offer Jennifer a whole wealth of new experiences, not only off the set, but also on. One of the most memorable was her first screen kiss.

"I had never kissed a boy before," she recalled, "so about fifteen minutes before we shot the scene, the director came and told the guy and I to go behind the bushes and kiss before we kissed on camera, so that we wouldn't be embarrassed. And so we did. So my first kiss in general was pretty weird."

She was, she told Jay Leno on the *Tonight* show, "scared half to death . . . and my mom was standing on the other side of the bushes! And the guy was like nineteen years old . . ."

It might not have been the most romantic moment for a first kiss, but at least the Hawaiian islands were a perfect setting. Jennifer Love Hewitt was growing up, along with the characters she was portraying.

". . . she came across as so angry and tempestuous," said Charles Eglee, one of the show's creators, in *TV Guide*. "Once I got to know her, I found she was one of the sweetest, most loving people."

Byrds of Paradise was a good show, well written and very well acted, with Jennifer a standout as a conflicted teen. The *Hollywood Reporter,* in a review, called it "a fresh, beautifully written, snappily acted, quality family drama," which made it a commodity rare on network television.

It faced two major problems. The first was the cost of producing it week after week. Location shooting was expensive, far more so than using a studio, but it was important to give the show a feeling of authenticity; it *had* to be made on Oahu.

The other big problem was the ratings. While it performed reasonably well, *Byrds of Paradise* didn't prove to be the immediate hit the network hoped it would be. Americans supposedly wanted both quality television and good family dramas, but when presented with one, they didn't flock to it in droves. It was an intelligent series, well above the lowest common denominator that seemed to pervade television, and that might well have worked against it. In the evenings people generally wanted to be mindlessly entertained, not to have to think; if they wanted to do that, PBS was just a click away.

So, at the end of its first season, the show was not renewed, much to the disappointment of cast and crew. For Jennifer, it had been her best experience yet, and, along with *Party of Five* (of course!), it still ranks as her favorite television acting. No reason was ever given for *Byrds of Paradise* being canceled. As Jennifer said, "I'm not sure why. We think it was because of the cost."

In actual fact, according to show creator Eglee, the show lost out because of the limited number of drama slots available. It came down to a choice between *Byrds of Paradise* and *My So-called Life,* with Claire Danes's show getting the final nod. Even though that show never did well in the ratings, either, being canceled after nineteen episodes, it did launch Danes's spectacular career.

For a couple of years, reruns of *Byrds of Paradise*

aired on cable's Family Channel, which offered another chance to watch the developing talents of Jennifer Love Hewitt.

So it was back to Los Angeles and home, the apartment she and Pat shared in Burbank. And home without work meant a return to regular school, to high school now, which proved even worse than her previous schooldays.

And Los Angeles also brought Love's first—and only—brush with the law. Perhaps inevitably, the cause of it all was a boy. They were parked on Mulholland Drive, supposedly to watch the lights of the city below. Instead, "we're, like, *really* making out and we had the heat on so the windows were all fogged up! We heard this knock, and a cop said, 'Roll down the window!' And I freaked out! I was like, 'Yes, Mr. Officer.' He said, 'What's going on in there?' I said, 'We're just making out. Very heavily, but just making out.' He said, 'I need you to get out of the car. Don't you know this is a restricted area?' I said, 'No, sir, I did not know that. I'm an actress and, see, actresses don't know these things. I have an early call in the morning and I *can't* be arrested.'"

She firmly believed that she was going to be hauled off to the police station for making out. The real problem was that they'd parked in the restricted area. Jennifer called her mom, expecting to be bawled out for indulging in a little passion. Instead, Pat just found the whole incident hilarious. She figured the scare had taught her daughter a much more powerful lesson than any she could pass on with words or punishment.

What Love needed was work. Her hopes had been so high for *Byrds of Paradise,* and she'd been crushed when it was canceled. She had been certain that would be the one.

Relief came quickly in the form of yet another series, this one starring televison veteran Chad Everett. *Mc-*

Kenna had him in the title role, as Jack McKenna, a man trying to keep his family together and his clothing business afloat.

After McKenna's son died—McKenna was a widower—his other, estranged son, Brick (Eric Close), returned home to help with the business, and also with his younger sister, Cassidy (Vanessa Shaw). Taking place in a small town in central Oregon (where it was filmed), the show offered both the outdoors and family drama. In other words, it was *Byrds of Paradise* meets *The Waltons* with action sequences, a different setting, and a slightly different theme. ABC, the network that had canceled *Byrds of Paradise*, picked up the show from its pilot, but wasn't happy with Shaw's portrayal of the standard troubled, rebellious teenage daughter. They wanted someone else.

After auditions, that someone else was Jennifer Love Hewitt. When the pilot aired in the fall of 1994, Shaw's performance was intact, but by the second episode, a week later, it was Love who was playing Cassidy.

In many ways it must have seemed like déjà vu to her. Her character was very similar to Franny Byrd, even if the dynamics of the fictional family were a little different.

Quite why ABC believed *McKenna* would succeed where *Byrds of Paradise* failed remains a mystery. Perhaps they thought that rock-climbing and river-rafting would bring in viewers who would normally shy away from a family drama. Whatever their reasoning, it was very soon apparent that this particular gamble wasn't going to pay off. *McKenna* stayed low in the ratings, and before it even had time to find its audience (assuming such a thing existed), the network yanked it from the air.

That meant Love was batting zero for three. Each of the series she'd been involved with had been a failure. She must have wondered briefly if she was some sort of jinx, and whether she was ever going to find her real place in television.

Once the shock and the new disappointment had worn off, and she'd returned to Los Angeles and the security of her apartment, she understood that this was simply the way the business worked. The majority of new series simply didn't make it. It was all a gamble, and she had to keep plugging away. She was barely sixteen; there was plenty of time yet, even if she didn't always feel that way.

Chapter Five

By the time *McKenna* was canceled, most series had already filmed their full seasons. *Party of Five* was among them, and its future hung in the balance. The cast and crew, not to mention the core of ardent fans the show had built up during its first season, were waiting breathlessly to hear if they'd have another chance to build an audience.

From the very beginning the show had seemed to teeter along from week to week. Even before it ever went on the air, it had seemed tenuous. The original idea, which had come from Sandy Grushow, who was then head of programming at the young FOX network, was for a series about kids living on their own, with none of the usual parental interference, something between *Beverly Hills 90210* and *Melrose Place,* with a hip, sexy edge.

Writers Christopher Keyser and Amy Lippman weren't too interested in something that bland. What they wanted to do, according to Lippman, was tell "a story about how the absence of parents affects children."

They took FOX's idea and put their own spin on it, creating the Salingers, three brothers and two sisters, ranging in age from one to twenty-four, whose restaurant-owning parents had died in an automobile accident six months prior to the show.

When they presented their script to FOX executives, Keyser and Lippman expected the worst. After all, the network hadn't built its reputation on drama. But they were given the green light to make the pilot episode.

The writers weren't the only ones who were apprehensive about the show, according to FOX development vice-president Bob Greenblatt: "We were nervous that it wasn't quite as high-concept, quite as cool and sexy as *90210*. We were thinking it should be more fun and light, while Chris and Amy really wanted to mine the dramatic side of it. But they were willing to do both, so we said, 'Go ahead.'"

Scott Wolf was the first actor cast, actually on the opening day of auditions.

"He's such a warm person that he seemed completely right for that character," said Lippman. Bailey was set.

Matthew Fox auditioned by video, and because of that he almost missed the part; there was a problem with either the tape or the lighting, leaving him looking distinctly green. But after Lippman and Keyser watched videos of some of his work, they had him flown to Los Angeles to audition in person.

"Once we saw him, that was sort of it," Lippman said. They had their Charlie.

Lacey Chabert too had auditioned by video. She worked onstage, and had been in television before, and simply had the sparkling intelligence the creators needed for Claudia. She was in.

The most difficult part to cast was that of Julia. Hundreds of actresses auditioned for the role, but FOX turned them all down. Time was running out. There were just two days left before filming was due to begin on the pilot. Then Neve Campbell walked in the door. She "read for two minutes and that was it," Keyser recalled. "We called the casting director and told her to book Neve immediately."

It was a case of perfect timing for Campbell. She'd been in Los Angeles, indeed in America, a little over a week. In her native Canada she'd had a great career, training as a dancer until an injury forced her to stop. Working as an actress, she'd done well, and even starred in a Canadian series, *Catwalk,* which turned her into something of a sex symbol. Her only reason for moving was the country itself.

"You get to a certain point in Canada, unfortunately, where you can only get so far and then you have to move to the States to get big," she explained. And now her chance to get big had arrived.

The entire cast, having signed five-year contracts, read for FOX executives, and passed with flying colors. It was February 1994, and there was a pilot show to be made.

Although the show was set in San Francisco, filming took place in Vancouver, British Columbia, returning Neve to Canada much sooner than she'd ever expected (although there was one day of filming in San Francisco, purely for exterior shots). It was simply much cheaper there than in Los Angeles. Everyone spent six weeks there, becoming close, bonding together like a real family.

In May 1994, FOX announced its schedule for the 1994–95 season, and *Party of Five* was on it, with thirteen episodes ordered. For the series proper the filming wouldn't take place in Canada, but on the Sony lot in Hollywood, with sets assembled on different soundstages. From Monday to Friday, the actors assembled at 6 A.M. for hair and makeup, finally able to go home at 8 P.M. (except for Chabert, who was legally limited to a ten-and-a-half-hour day). And once every week, just like the fictional Salingers, the cast would get together for a meal, a different member hosting each time.

They were more than actors working together; they quickly became friends. In spite of its frequent dark drama onscreen, the set of *Party of Five* was a place of laughter.

"We're always being told, 'Okay guys, settle down,'" Chabert related. "We have too much fun. When someone laughs, that's it. We're all gone."

From the beginning, the show had the critics on its side. In the *New York Post,* John Podhoretz wrote, "FOX's *Party of Five* is hands-down the best pilot of the upcoming fall season. It's a terrifically intelligent, emotionally restrained drama . . . and it is beautifully acted by a cast of unknowns."

That was high praise. All it needed was for plaudits like that to translate into viewers. Unfortunately, it didn't. In its first few weeks, airing on Monday nights at 9 P.M., *Party of Five* stayed in the bottom ten of the ratings for prime-time shows. People simply weren't tuning in. Most networks would have quickly abandoned something so blatantly unsuccessful, but FOX worked a little differently. They were willing to give it time. After all, two of their biggest shows, *Melrose Place* and *Beverly Hills 90210,* hadn't caught on immediately.

Finally, FOX agreed to try the show on a Wednesday, following *Beverly Hills 90210*. It helped, but only to the extent of one rating point, hardly what everyone had hoped. Both cast and crew began to wonder about their future. FOX had ordered three more episodes shot, and scripts written for the rest of the season, but that still didn't mean any guarantees.

Everyone was frustrated, as Scott Wolf explained. "You start to think, 'Am I pouring my heart into something that will be gone next week?'"

Still, in November came some measure of relief—the show was picked up for the rest of the season. Nevertheless no one was breathing much easier.

In January 1995, *Party of Five* made a permanent

transition to Wednesday nights, and things did improve. The ratings increased, most notably with the eighteen-to-thirty-four age group, a demographic the advertisers loved. But improvements were relative. The show was still very far from setting the world on fire, and the critics, who still loved the show, predicted the worst.

It was the viewers who saved it, really. *TV Guide* organized their annual "Save Our Shows" poll, and *Party of Five* garnered 28,000 votes. The Gay and Lesbian Alliance Against Defamation sent out postcards for the members to mail to FOX, labeled "Don't Stop the Party." And the Internet, still very much in its fledgling days, was used by fans to spread the good word.

It was a prodigious effort, but it paid off in May, when FOX announced that the show would be renewed for a second season, actually the lowest-rated prime-time show ever to have made the cut.

Still, it needed support, and it got that from any number of sources. *TV Guide* used a cover story to name it "The Best Series You're Not Watching," and *People, Time,* and *USA Today* put it in the category of the year's best television. The award of a Golden Globe for Best Television Drama in January 1996 further put the spotlight on the show.

The show had made it into a second season, quite deservedly. But, as with any show, there were changes to be made. Not in the Salingers themselves—those would come through the ongoing storylines—but with the addition of some characters. What they needed was another teenage girl, one the same age as Julia, but very different in personality, who could become a possible love interest for Bailey. Keyser and Lippman even had a name for her: Sarah Reeves. Now all they needed was someone to play her.

Love hadn't paid much attention to *Party of Five*; there simply hadn't been the time to watch television. She was back in regular school, which she hated with a passion.

"The kids just thought I was some freak and tried to beat me up. I used to get Coke thrown on me."

But she also had her other life. There were auditions, and something new, something the girls who hated her would never have. She had a recording contract.

She already knew she was a good singer, and she'd made demo tapes, which her agent had circulated to record companies. Since she concentrated on her acting, and was working hard to find another good role, she didn't follow what was happening with the tapes too closely. Until her agent called and told her she had a record deal!

Her first record, in 1992, had done very well in Japan, of course, but later she'd more or less disowned it as being very childish. Now she was being offered the chance to record again, in the United States, and for one of the biggest of the major labels—Atlantic. Could it get any better than that?

As it turned out, the answer was yes. Her auditions had been fruitless lately. She arrived home one evening with Pat, tired, to find pages of dialogue in her fax machine, along with an audition date. The script's heading was "PO5," which meant nothing to her, and she wondered what it could be. Then she sat down and read the words.

Party of Five was casting for the role of Sarah Reeves, and once Love had read through the scene, she knew she'd been born to play Sarah.

"I was like, 'Wow, this character talks exactly like me!' I knew how to play her instantly."

The audition was just two days away. She didn't even have to think about what to wear, but went as herself, in a T-shirt and jeans, wearing next to no makeup. As soon as she arrived at the studio, however, she began to wonder if she was doing the right thing.

"I walked in and there were twenty-five-year-olds in little tight dresses with lots of makeup and hair. They were beautiful, tall, and model-looking. I came in jeans and a little T-shirt and I looked ten next to them. I'm thinking, 'Oh, right! Like I stand a chance.' "

But this wasn't an audition for *Melrose Place*. Keyser and Lippman wanted someone real, someone believable as Sarah, not a cookie-cutter gorgeous-actress type. And acting ability was every bit as important as the look.

Love knew Sarah *was* her, and once she'd read the scene, she had the producers believing it, too. This was a role she really wanted, that meant a lot to her, although she knew nothing about the show, and it came across in her audition. Everyone was impressed by her performance, so much so that they were willing to alter their vision of the character to make it more like Love herself. A few days later she received the call she'd been waiting and hoping for—she had the part of Sarah Reeves. There was nothing else to do but run screaming around the apartment.

"I actually didn't think I would get the part, and was very pleasantly surprised when I did. And very thankful."

Co-executive producer Ken Topolsky made it apparent why she'd been the obvious choice to play Sarah when he praised her talents.

"She's probably the most talented young actress I've ever worked with," he said. "She has incredible instincts, she has incredible talent, she takes direction well. She's smart. She's a special actress."

And she was about to become a full member of the *Party of Five* family. First, though, she had to concentrate on finishing her record, which would include one of her own compositions. The album, to be titled (unfortunately) *Let's Go Bang,* was set for release late in 1995—perfect timing, since Love would then be very visible from her appearances on *Party of Five*.

"That title [*Let's Go Bang*] was a mistake," she laughed. "I loved the song and 'the bang' was a dance. It was supposed to be like the 'Electric Slide' kind of thing. It wasn't promoted so some people thought I was some perverted sixteen-year-old."

Although it hadn't been, and wouldn't be, the real focus of her career, Love was very definitely passionate about her music. Singing was the first thing she'd done as a performer, and it still occupied a very special place in her heart.

"Singing comes from my soul and my gut," she explained, "and there's nothing else like it." She was in love, not just with singing, but music in general. "My radio is timed to turn on the minute I wake up and I listen to CDs every single day, all day long."

Recording her album, finding the time for it as she began working on the character of Sarah Reeves, put Love under a great deal of pressure. Instead of focusing on one thing or the other, she had to split her time between the two. Both were incredible opportunities for her, and she wasn't about to blow either of them. And there was a third ingredient added to this stew: fame. *Party of Five* might not have scored highly in the ratings during its first season, but it was definitely high-profile. And that meant that Love was, too.

"I remember the first time I walked through a press line. I had just been cast on *Party of Five*. The photographers were like, 'What's her name?'"

Being an unknown would not last long. Soon enough, perhaps even sooner than she'd anticipated, she'd be a star. But not everywhere. One big marketing mistake on the part of the record label was that *Let's Go Bang* really wasn't promoted to take advantage of her new TV visibility. Instead Atlantic simply let the album slide into oblivion, with no push, and next to no airplay. That was a big shame, given that Love had made a very good record.

"People have said that I sound like a cross between Mariah Carey and Toni Braxton," she said, "but it's me!"

It was pop music, with a definite R&B tip, and showed a girl who was really growing into her voice, and who knew how to use it. Prior to the sessions, she'd worked with a vocal coach. She had the notes and the tone, but there was still work to be done on her breathing and intonation, and on learning to make the most of her natural talents.

She'd grown up listening to the sixties music her mother played, which had been a big influence, and from there she had gravitated to R&B.

"I grew up on Janis Joplin, Aretha Franklin, the Shirelles, so the older stuff is my favorite music," she explained in an America Online chat. "But probably my favorite music of today is, I would have to go with R&B."

Even though she'd started out by singing country, and that family link with Patsy Cline meant it was somewhere in her genes, it was no longer really a part of her musically.

"I grew up singing it, and heard it so much growing up, that I've sort of grown out of it," Love explained.

Actually, the comparisons to Mariah Carey aren't that strange. While Love's voice isn't as refined, and certainly doesn't have the range of Carey's, it is more than just pleasant. It has personality and emotion, everything she needs to put a song across, something her acting and performing experience have helped with. And romantic songs seem to come naturally to her.

"I don't know if I like singing about it the most, but mostly what I sing about is love, because I'm a hopeless romantic, so I tend to pick songs that are very romantic."

Let's Go Bang had plenty of songs on a romantic tip, mixed in with dancier tracks, like the title song. It really came as something of a surprise to anyone who'd come to know Love through her acting.

The cover was *definitely* a different side of JLH. With her hair teased and looking very sultry, showing those big brown eyes and full lips, this was sexy. And the silver bra and midriff-baring stretch pants only added to that image. This wasn't Robin from *Kids Incorporated,* and it definitely wasn't Sarah Reeves, although a sticker on the cover pointed out that she was the new "star" of *Party of Five.* Inside the CD booklet, there were more pictures of her, one of which was very glamorous: her face pale, hair parted to the side, she lay on the floor in a dress . . . very different. Even in the most ordinary picture, of Love wearing jeans, her hair was teased—which really didn't suit her, since it made her look like a refugee from the eighties.

Let's Go Bang had been produced by Angelo Montrone, who also contributed a couple of songs and took care of all the keyboards. Most of the players were session people, although Sheila E, who'd once played with Prince, contributed percussion to the title track. Although the music had been recorded at twelve studios on the east and west coasts, Jennifer's vocals had all been laid down at Red Zone Studios, close to home in Burbank.

It was her singing that was meant to impress, and it definitely did. She handled not only all the lead vocals, but also most of the backgrounds, which in some ways was trickier, building up track after track to get harmonies that fitted just perfectly.

For a sixteen-year-old, Love had an incredibly mature voice. When people had said it was a cross between Mariah Carey and Toni Braxton, that was quite close to the truth—and the same thing could have been said of the material, too. She was confident, and even sultry at times, on both the up-tempo material and the ballads. This was someone who was comfortable with her voice (although she did thank her vocal coach, Seth Riggs, for his help), and who knew how to use it expressively.

That was obvious right from the start of the first track, "Kiss Away From Heaven," with its strong dance beat, and some great deep bass propelling everything along. JLH was in full control of the lyric, soaring over the top. Like almost every track on the record, this could easily have stood alone as a single: catchy, with a great chorus and hook that Love delivered like a knockout blow.

The title track, "Let's Go Bang," saw the girl getting very funky. Sheila E's percussion seemed to lead the music, and it was easy to picture Jennifer up on a stage, getting a crowd to move and dance—an idea enhanced by the audience applauding at the end. While she might have seemed more like a wistful balladeer, these two cuts made it apparent that she could do just about anything and deliver the goods.

"The Difference Between Us" did slow the groove, though, but only down to mid-pace, letting Love emote. More than anything else, this was a song that made you think of Mariah Carey; it was something that could easily have been on one of her albums, and Jennifer actually did it as much justice as Mariah would have, wrapping herself around a romantic lyric and really getting to the heart of the song.

She slowed the tempo even further for "Couldn't Find Another Man," which was addressed to that perfect boyfriend, one she didn't have yet in real life. But that wasn't about to stop her imagining on a ballad, where she managed to sound so dreamy it was impossible to believe that she wasn't looking ahead and picturing the right man in her mind.

Then the album took a very jazzy turn with "You Make Me Smile," which seemed a little awkward at first, pitched slightly differently from everything that had gone before it. It soon found its stride, however. Like almost everything else on *Let's Go Bang*, it was a love song, and a reminder that love was supposed to make you happy, not angst-ridden and sad.

It was only right that a record like this had at least one big, dramatic ballad where Love could really sing, and "In Another Life" was actually the first of two. While she couldn't quite stretch to diva octaves, she showed that she really could capture a romantic lyric and push it, in this case over a large, swooping string section. Anyone who'd thought that Jennifer was still a girl would have had second thoughts after this. She sounded completely adult, ready to take on the world. And why not? This disc was her big opportunity to do just that. Every cut was a way to prove herself, to show that she could sing as well as, if not better than, anyone else.

She really seemed more comfortable on the slower songs than the dance material, oddly enough, perhaps because they gave her more chance to wring the emotion from a lyric. But "Can't Stand in the Way of Love" worked as the best dance song on the record, perhaps because it was a little more understated—it didn't try to throw everything into the mix.

The real highlight of the album, though, was "Free to Be a Woman," for which Love had written the lyrics. Unlike the others, this wasn't a love song, but more like the idea of the Spice Girls' "Wannabe" ahead of its time. If a boy was interested in checking out her body, she sang, first he should take a look at her mind. She had no wish to be shackled into the roles people thought women should have, and she didn't see why any other girls should be, either. Very different from the poetry she loved to write (some of which has appeared on JLH Web sites), this song was quite political in its own way, and being sung over a very catchy tune didn't hurt. It offered a glimpse into Love's deepest thoughts, and underscored the fact that by now she really was a woman, one who wanted, and deserved, to be taken seriously. It was something she'd obviously thought about a great deal before putting anything on paper, and the way she sang the song made it apparent that it meant a lot to her.

Then it was time to chill with a couple more ballads. "Everywhere I Go" was again reminiscent of Mariah Carey—in many ways she was the main reference point for the whole album—and the kind of song that suited her so perfectly, with a slight bounce to the beat, the kind of song that left you smiling when it was over.

"Don't Turn Your Head Away" once again brought in the full string section, pulling out all the stops on a big number that she carried off with great ease, emotional and stirring in its intensity, letting the spotlight fall squarely on her voice.

To round things off, there was an odd cover of Bread's 1971 hit, "Baby I'm-a Want You," which had originally been a ballad, but in this version put a real swing in the beat, and a sax solo over the top, as well as using the background vocals (one of the two tracks on the record where Jennifer didn't contribute to the harmonies) to full effect on the bridge. Even if it wasn't the most successful cover of the tune, which didn't really lend itself to a swing beat, it still made for a pleasant ending to the album.

All in all, it was something of a triumph. It showed not only that she could sing, but sing very well, indeed. The little girl who'd made her first album three years before was now all grown-up and very womanly. The songs, if not the cover image, were something that were really *her,* that showed her romantic side to full effect.

It was proof that Love was definitely in the house, and ready to be taken seriously. And she should have been. She'd put out an excellent album, one which deserved to be widely heard, and which could have spawned a few hit singles, if things went right.

The crime, perhaps, was that this record simply wasn't promoted. It had all the ingredients of a major hit, with good, catchy songs and an excellent singer. And with Love appearing on *Party of Five,* the label had plenty to capitalize on. Instead *Let's Go Bang* was pushed out of the nest to fly or fall; another teen voice that someone, somewhere, might just listen to.

With no publicity, there was no way for fans to even realize the record was in the stores, and so it didn't really sell. No airplay, no interviews, just another CD in the racks.

However, Love had made an album, and that was a major achievement. She could look at it, listen to it, and know that she'd done it, created something really worthwhile. Of course it hurt that *Let's Go Bang* didn't sell, but the record was still a solid accomplishment, much more so than the first record, which had been little more than the work of a kid—as she admitted herself. *Let's Go Bang* was a woman's album, and Jennifer saw herself as a woman now—after all, hadn't she written the track "Free to Be a Woman"?

More to the point, Atlantic Records didn't drop her, even though the sales of the record were poor. They'd thrown it out there, and not done much to help it along, but the simple fact was that Jennifer Love Hewitt was gaining an audience for herself through *Party of Five.* Previously she'd just been another kid in a television series, but this show was different. She had her own fans now, as *Party of Five* gained in popularity. And that meant that in a year or so, another record could do much better . . .

It was the type of convoluted thinking that typified the record business, however. In truth, it looked as if they hadn't known what to do with Jennifer on this release. The songs were adult, but the image they gave her on the cover, sexy as it was, seemed to be of a little vixen, too contrived to ever be real. Certainly it confused the new fans who were coming to know her through the character of Sarah. Love with teased hair and silver bras wasn't what they were expecting.

"As far as the sexy clothing on the cover," she explained, "it probably appeared more so because on the show I'm so played down—hair-, makeup-, and wardrobe-wise."

Instead of letting her be herself, Atlantic Records clearly couldn't decide what to do with her, or even where to pitch her, and the album ended up falling through the cracks. Still, at least Jennifer would have another opportunity.

But for now she needed to totally focus on the acting aspect of her career. This, she felt, could be the break she'd been waiting for and working toward for years. Blowing it was the last thing she wanted to do.

Chapter Six

By the start of filming for the second season of *Party of Five,* all the people involved really did resemble a family. They'd already survived a great deal together, barely knowing from week to week whether the show would be canceled. With a lot of help and support from viewers and critics, they'd made it through, but they also knew that FOX couldn't stick with them forever unless things began to improve. And improve they would: in January 1996, *Party of Five* was awarded a Golden Globe as Best Drama Series, which brought more curious viewers into the fold. Some of them stayed. The addition of the venerable Carroll O'Connor (*All in the Family, In the Heat of the Night*) in a recurring role as the Salinger grandfather also helped to boost ratings. The show had begun the season with a thirteen-episode commitment from FOX, a good start but not a sign of unconditional acceptance. On February 29, 1996, the network renewed it for a third season, allowing everyone involved with *Party of Five* to breathe a little more easily.

It would have been perfectly understandable if they'd been wary of newcomers, people brought in to beef up the cast and add a touch of romantic sizzle to the storylines—people like Love. Instead, everyone welcomed her with open arms. In particular, Scott Wolf (Bailey) went out of his way to make her feel at home.

"Every morning he takes time to make you feel special—whether it's giving you a hug, or saying, 'Wow, you look nice today,'" she remembered.

Love's character, Sarah Reeves, would be a regular on the show, along with Justin Thompson (Michael Goorjian), and Griffin Holbrook (Jeremy London). Love and London had, in fact, met before, when they were both auditioning for the film *Mallrats,* Kevin Smith's skewed teen pic, which was supposed to launch a movie career for *Beverly Hills 90210* queen Shannen Doherty. London had definitely noticed her at the audition—his major disappointment was that she was only fifteen, a bit too young.

Sarah Reeves was supposed to be a friend of Julia Salinger's (Neve Campbell), and a classmate of hers. As the season opened, she'd spent the summer working at Salinger's, partly for the money—although the Reeveses weren't short of cash, by any means—but mostly to be close to Bailey, on whom she had a massive crush.

Like Love herself, Sarah was a girl who was eager to please, especially if the person to be pleased was Bailey. She was head over heels in love with him. The only problem was that Bailey was still recovering from the cocaine overdose death of his former girlfriend, Jill (Megan Ward), who died at the end of the first season. He didn't have a clue as to Sarah's feelings for him, no matter how obvious she tried to make them. Part of the problem was that Sarah was just *so* eager to please, so quick to help Bailey, that she was almost a doormat.

When he decided to run for class vice-president, in the season's third episode, it was Sarah who rushed to become his campaign manager, simply for the opportunity to spend more time with him. Bailey, though, wasn't that interested in school politics; he simply wanted to enhance his transcript.

Inevitably, it was poor Sarah who ended up doing all the work for Bailey. And, typically unthinking, he let her, not even noticing how much she was doing, until it all came to a head and she told him that the real reason she'd undertaken all this was because she was in love with him. That at least made him sit up and think a little, although, being Bailey, not too long, and not too hard.

Her new visibility on the show was a big boost for Love. She had a great character, great scripts and storylines, and suddenly people knew just who she was, after she'd worked so hard for six years in television. The fact that she'd become known really hit home for her one day when she stopped for a Slurpee at a 7-Eleven near her house, and ran into two of the girls who'd made her life so miserable at school the year before.

"I got that old fear back, like, 'Oh, my God.' Then they came up to me and they said, 'We just love *Party of Five.* Would you mind signing something?' And I said, 'You know what? I'm sorry, I can't. I have to go. Really nice to see you. Bye-bye.' I wanted to say something really mean, but why go to their level."

It really meant something that these girls would come up to her like fans now. After years of being taunted in regular school, she'd proved something to everyone, that she could make it, and that acting could be worthwhile, as could singing.

Of course, working for a living didn't mean she could ignore school. She was a junior now, but was tutored on the set, along with Lacey Chabert, the only other regular member of the cast who was under eighteen.

While those who were of age worked long, long days, usually twelve to fourteen hours each day, Monday to Friday, Jennifer and Lacey were limited to ten and a half hours on the set, part of which had to be devoted to their schooling.

"I do my school . . . either in between scenes or I'll come in before my scenes and do my three hours of school," Jennifer recounted.

She quickly settled into the routine and the atmosphere of the show. The drama might have come on hot and heavy on television, but as she soon discovered, the set was nothing but fun.

"[A]nybody that would come to our set would think that we are the sickest, most demented people ever. You have never heard so much laughter coming from our set. Neve and I aren't really allowed to do scenes together anymore, because we cause so much trouble ... We all have a really, really good time, and believe it or not the emotional stuff that we get to do is why, if you meet the cast, we're some of the happiest, bubbliest people you'd want to meet."

But they could get serious and professional when necessary, and then they were grateful for such excellent scripting.

"[W]e have such great writers that very rarely do any of us have any problems with things that we're saying," Jennifer explained, "and if we do, they're little things, like we just don't feel like our character would say that. So if that happens, the writers are very good about letting us change the words to feel a little better."

One thing the writers weren't about to change was the tortured relationship between Sarah and Bailey. On one level they were so similar, both needy, but Bailey was afraid to show that side of himself. For Sarah, though, it was almost her reason for living. When Bailey seriously injured his teammate in football practice, Sarah was the one who was there for him, to comfort him and try to banish all the bad thoughts.

But there were limits to what she could take. When his behavior became very erratic, as he tried to make his relationship with Sarah into a duplicate of the one he'd enjoyed with Jill before she died, Sarah had no choice but to break things off. She didn't want to walk that self-destructive path.

In real life, the course of true love for Jennifer wasn't

running much smoother. She thought she'd found the man of her dreams. The problem was that, like Bailey, he hadn't found her yet.

On October 3, 1995, Jennifer Love went out on a blind date. She'd been set up by a friend with a boy from the neighborhood. Very close in the neighborhood, since it turned out that Will Friedle lived literally half a block away. He was virtually the boy next door.

"When we went out, we hit it off, but Will kept bringing up the fact that he was three years older than I was. After the date, I said to myself, 'That was my prince.'"

It seemed that the age gap kept Will from thinking of her as his princess, unfortunately. But Love couldn't get him out of her mind. Two weeks later she still hadn't heard anything from him. She wanted to phone him but didn't have his number, and didn't want to appear desperate by asking their mutual friend for it. Instead, "I called Will from the intercom outside his apartment building. I left a message asking him to the movies."

It was a very nineties thing to do, but then again, she was a very nineties girl. If she wanted something, she was going to go for it. And she had, she'd done what she could. All she could do now was sit back and wait for Will. If he wasn't interested, he'd call her back. After all, even if she was younger, she was a woman, and she had a lot going for her. She knew they had a lot in common, she knew there was a real connection between them.

Either Will was blind to all that, or he was really scared of it. He never did call her back. She'd made her move, put herself on the line, and he'd rejected her. She felt bad, because she knew they could have had something really good. But there was nothing more she could do about it.

A few weeks passed, and still there was no word from Will. Instead someone else asked her out—actor

Joey Lawrence, who was quite a hunk in his own right, and who, like Love, was also a singer. They seemed to have a lot in common. Everything was cool again.

On *Party of Five*, Sarah had become a regular cast member, with as many emotional highs and lows as any of the Salingers. Bailey, unwilling to commit to Sarah, gave his friend Will permission to date her. However, when Bailey saw them out together, it just tore him apart. He wanted her, but he didn't want her, too.

"I think Bailey and Sarah are soulmates," Love mused. "In a lot of ways they are very much the male and female version of each other. They are both very strong. They're both people who make it their daily job to make sure that other people around them are taken care of and happy. They think of themselves last. And they love each other."

It might have been a tortured kind of love, but they did love each other, even if it wasn't always evident. There was a definite bond between the two of them. They shared a very human, very real relationship right from the beginning. For a rich girl, Sarah showed a remarkable amount of vulnerability.

"One of the great things about Sarah is that she has to figure out how to survive with the mistakes she makes and get herself back on track," Love explained. "And there isn't a person in the universe who doesn't make mistakes."

One thing that Sarah believed wasn't a mistake was her desire, her love, for Bailey. Finally, in December 1995, in the episode where Charlie and Kirsten were supposed to get married, Sarah and Bailey finally kissed and got together.

"I get a lot of hate mail about that," Jennifer said. "I do. I get a lot of mail that starts off 'We hate you' ... but then by the end of it, it's like, 'But we're glad if he's going to have a girlfriend, it's you.' So it's kind of nice."

Finally, it seemed, things were going to go smoothly. Certainly, compared to the girls in Bailey's past, Sarah was a dream. She was down-to-earth, took nothing for granted, and had no apparent bad habits.

Her turn at trauma was to come the very next week, though, when Sarah accidentally discovered that she was adopted, and the Reeves family wasn't her "real" family. Inevitably, it set her wondering just who she was, who her mother had been, and why she was the way she was, what traits she might have inherited. As she was approaching her sixteenth birthday, she was questioning everything about the world, anyway. To have this burden on top of everything else was the last thing she needed.

To do something, to burn off all her feelings, Sarah embarked on a spending spree, as if she were trying to get rid of all the money her adoptive parents had given her. The chronically short-of-cash Bailey found this disturbing. Sarah was privileged—she could afford almost anything she wanted—but she was normally so restrained. It worried Bailey to see her so reckless. It also worried Mr. and Mrs. Reeves, who could only believe that Sarah was trying to punish them for never having told her she was adopted. To them, though, she was their real daughter. They'd raised her and loved her when her biological mother couldn't, and they realized that there was a lot more to being a parent than just giving birth.

At the same time, they thought expensive gifts could say a lot, which wasn't always the case. For Sarah's sixteenth birthday, their gift to her was a brand-new red convertible—the kind of car any teenager (and most adults) would find cool. And it was. But it didn't mean anywhere near as much to her as Bailey's gift. With no money to match what the Reeveses would give their daughter, he had to use his imagination. He had a star named after her, about as romantic a thing as Bailey

Salinger would ever do, and it was a gesture that Sarah simply loved.

Sarah was about ready to flex her wings a little, to try new things, and one of them was singing (which was perfectly natural for Love, of course). But it caused tension and arguments among the Salingers when Bailey, fighting with Julia for the attic room in the house, encouraged Sarah to follow her ambitions and audition for a band, the Nielsens (named for television's Nielsen ratings). That was a gig Julia desperately wanted, but Sarah, the better singer, was accepted.

Sarah was coming to terms with the fact that she'd been adopted, but she was still curious to know who her real mother was, quite understandably. After overhearing a comment, she began to look for her birth mother, not knowing what she might find. Would the woman accept her with open arms? Would they be very much alike?

Bailey also began searching for Sarah's mother, and with a lot more success. He actually found her, only to learn that the woman had no wish to dredge up the past and meet her daughter. How would he tell that to Sarah, though? About all he could do was lie, and hope she'd never find the woman herself. Luckily for him, the levelheaded Sarah realized it would all be a waste of time anyway, and decided to give up the hunt and get on with her life.

Even so, she was at a fragile stage. That fragility wasn't helped when Robin (Patricia Heaton), her real mother, had a change of heart and suddenly introduced herself, turning Sarah's world upside down. Robin was a musician, and about to leave on tour for half a year. To have someone so important come into her life and then vanish again disoriented Sarah, and that feeling was compounded when Bailey announced he was going to college in Boston. Sarah was totally without any of the bearings and anchors she relied on, and in severe danger of losing it.

Bailey, who really cared for Sarah, then decided to go to a college in California to remain near her, but Sarah, coming to her senses, realized that he had his own life to live, and told him that he should go to Boston.

Bailey had always had great difficulty being romantic—his birthday gift to Sarah had been the exception, not the rule, and it had come about because he was low on cash—and his Valentine's Day present to her showed him at his worst. He took her to a monster truck show. Needless to say, she wasn't impressed, preferring the poetic company of her neighbor, Sean (Ivan Sergei). In a fit of jealousy, assuming a romance between the two of them, Bailey hit Sean, leaving Sarah wondering if Bailey really was the right man for her.

But they didn't break up—far from it. Instead they were about to get physical, and consummate their relationship. Bailey had bought condoms, and they believed they were ready. And they would have been, until Julia told Sarah about her pregnancy, and her decision to have an abortion. Julia needed to talk, she needed a friend, but this was one situation where Sarah couldn't provide a shoulder for someone to cry on. As an adopted child, she felt abortion was wrong, and couldn't counsel Julia.

It did make Sarah think deeply about what she and Bailey were about to do, however, and she ended up having second thoughts, and a case of cold feet. It was too big a step, and she simply wasn't ready yet. Sex was a real commitment for her, and she needed to find herself first.

Part of doing that was by singing with the Nielsens, who, thanks to Bailey, had a gig at Salinger's Restaurant. But Bailey was more than a little surprised and shocked when Sarah appeared for the show looking . . . sexy. This wasn't the girl he knew, and he didn't want people ogling her. He tried to tell her how she should dress, even what songs she ought to sing, but she wasn't about to listen to him. She was exploring the possibilities of herself, and it was something she needed to do on her own.

As the season ended, everything was in flux. Sarah was mugged, which brought out Bailey's protective streak. He became overly concerned with her safety, handling everything as badly as possible. She needed breathing room, and he was smothering her. But when she raised the issue, he reacted in a typically hurt-male fashion. He offered her all the space she wanted—by breaking up with her.

It was all bluster and bravado, not even a real breakup as it turned out. But of course, by having said the words, he couldn't take them back; there was too much pride involved. And there were other issues in his life. The Salingers were in grave danger of losing their restaurant. Without the help of grandfather Jake (Carroll O'Connor) they would have. But the money he gave them to save Salinger's was money he'd planned on using to pay Bailey's college tuition in Boston. So, after all, Bailey had no option but to attend a state college. And just now, that suited him perfectly, since it kept him near Sarah.

Her first season on *Party of Five* had been a great success for Love, and not just because the show hadn't been canceled, although that was a first for her. Its ratings had improved, and it had become something of a cult show for young viewers. Now, a lot of people knew her face and her name, which was gratifying, since she'd worked long and hard to reach that stage. On top of that, she'd had some great scripts, lots of meat for an actress. In other words, the show had proved to be everything she could have hoped for. Suddenly, as an actress she was very visible. It seemed she was finally starting to live the dream she'd had for so long.

Chapter Seven

Even though the previous few months had been exhausting, Love wasn't necessarily about to give herself a break. If anything, she was going to spend the time away from *Party of Five* working harder than ever. While the show was on "summer" (actually early spring) break she was lined up to make not one, but two movies, and also work on her next album, more than enough for one girl to undertake.

The first thing on the agenda was *House Arrest*, a movie starring Jamie Lee Curtis, whose name was quite bankable after her appearance as Arnold Schwarzenegger's wife in the action-comedy *True Lies*.

Actually, for JLH life was never as simple as just having *one* thing on the agenda. Even as she started work on the movie, she was beginning sessions for the album that would come out later that year under the simple title *Jennifer Love Hewitt*. The schedule was shattering, and meant that she'd be driven from the set to the studio, while trying to get some sleep in the car.

The absolute highlight of *House Arrest* for her was working with Curtis.

"She is one of the coolest ladies I've ever met. Very funny, very sweet, an experience I wouldn't trade for anything in the world," Love said later. It could have been that her attitude was colored a little by some of Curtis's actions, though. Since there was no break for teen actors, Love had to be tutored—along with many others in the cast—on the set. Curtis "would come into school and tell us she needed to talk to us, and sneak us candy. She's so real, and she has no idea how special she is. She was so nice to me."

For a brief while, however, it was debatable whether Love would actually be in the cast.

"Originally they said I looked a little too old," she explained. "The character is thirteen and they were afraid I might be a little too mature-looking to play thirteen. So I came back with like no makeup on, my hair a little curly because curly tends to look younger, played down my clothes a bit, and I got the movie."

Working with Curtis gave her a thrill—especially when at Christmas, long, long after the shoot was done, Curtis called to wish her happy holidays—but she was also looking forward to working with Jennifer Tilly, who'd play her mom.

"As Brooke, I'm supposed to be embarrassed by her, but all I kept thinking was, 'My mom was nominated for an Oscar!'"

The movie really centered around fourteen-year-old Grover Beindorf (Kyle Howard), his younger sister Stacy, and their parents (Jamie Lee Curtis, Kevin Pollak). Even as they celebrated their eighteenth anniversary, the Beindorfs told their kids that they were separating. Grover's friend Matt, who'd been through this himself, suggested locking them in a closet to work things out, but Grover took the idea one stage further. Holding an anniversary party for their parents in the basement, the kids locked them in there. They had previously boarded up the windows and blocked every means of escape.

The next day, in the boys' bathroom at school, Grover told Matt what he'd done. But he was overheard by TJ, the school bully who'd made Grover's life such a misery. TJ, though, was impressed, so much so that he turned up later at the Beindorf house, and fitted a new iron security door to the basement.

That was far from the extent of his involvement. He kidnapped his parents, who were having their problems, and Matt's parents, who joined the crowd in the basement, while the kids (and their pets, including a bulldog and a snake) moved in upstairs.

Grover tried to keep a handle on things. He wanted to conduct group therapy sessions for the parents; the aim, after all, was to keep them together. He even went to the library to do some research. There he saw Brooke Figler (Jennifer Love Hewitt), who began to cry. The next thing you knew, her mother, Cindy (Jennifer Tilly), was over at the Beindorfs' joining the basement crew. Her problem wasn't a marriage, but the fact that she tried to look, act, and sound like her teenage daughter.

The kids kept a video camera trained on their parents, and microphones helped communication between floors. In many ways, the kids were acting more maturely than the adults, even as they had fun. But the adults began to loosen up a little, too. They plotted a means of escape, through the boarded-up laundry chute. Curtis climbed up the chute, her face appearing in front of the kids in the bedroom before she tumbled back down.

It seemed as if the couples in the basement were getting closer, until a lawyer brought the divorce papers Mrs. Beindorf planned to serve on her husband. For him, separating had been a reluctant option, and he hadn't even considered divorce. Meanwhile, Grover and Brooke were getting closer. It was apparent that she not only liked him but respected him.

Finally the men managed to break through the cement covering one window, and sent Matt's father (Wallace Shawn) out. The only problem was that he couldn't make it all the way. Nor could the kids push him back down.

All the activity spurred the former chief of police, who lived across the street, to call in the cops, and they arrived in force, even bringing a SWAT team. What choice did the kids have but to surrender? So the parents were free. But it had had an effect. Matt's father and stepmom stayed together, and even had another child. Brooke's mother grew up. TJ's parents did divorce, but after his mother finished law school, they formed a business partnership. And Grover's parents? They managed to work things out.

The kids became school celebrities. Grover got the girl, and he and Stacy went with their parents on their second honeymoon to Hawaii. In the end, everyone lived happily ever after.

So it was typical lightweight teen fare. As long as it entertained, what else mattered? It was funny, showed the kids as smarter than the adults, and put a good spin on what has always been a difficult situation, particularly for kids, who are usually powerless when parents split up. Showing them taking control, and helping to affect their parents' decisions, was only a good thing.

It was a comedy, and strictly played for laughs, but there were also some underlying lessons and a bit of food for thought. When the kids sat down for dinner and tried champagne, they all spat it back out, hating the taste. And it did offer the message that sometimes adults do split up too easily, do quit trying and take what seems like the easy option of divorce.

Love's part was relatively minor. She was a mixture of house mother to the kids and also the token babe, the romantic interest for Grover. But it was good exposure for her. Her career was moving along steadily. And, as she well knew, there was nothing wrong with being a supporting actress. Being part of a team, a cast, working as an ensemble, was what acting was all about.

She'd decided a couple of years before, and told Pat Hewitt, that she didn't want to have the lead in anything until she was eighteen, that she wouldn't be ready for it before then. At that point the pressure would really be on her to perform, to carry a movie or a television show, and she didn't need that yet. She had enough on her plate just coping with everything, let alone having to deal with *that* stress.

The new album she was recording for Atlantic, the one to be known as *Jennifer Love Hewitt*, was proving to be quite different from the record she'd made the year before. It was decidedly softer, on much more of an R&B tip, taking advantage of Love's sultry, slightly husky voice by placing it on a lot of mid-paced songs.

She was growing up at a rapid rate. On this disc no one would be going bang, and no one would be getting loud and funky. In retrospect, that was probably a good thing. Something a little quieter and more intimate suited her style much more, and projected her warmth.

Apart from timing, what linked this record to *House Arrest* was the song JLH sang in the film, "It's Good to Know I'm Alive," which was included as a "bonus track" on *Jennifer Love Hewitt*. Perhaps wisely, it was stuck right at the end. Good as it was, it completely broke the album's mood, poppy and bouncy after the more late-night feel of the other eleven tracks.

The record saw Jennifer paired with a number of different producers, many of whom were also songwriters who contributed their work. In fact, apart from Love, the album's only consistent element was Valerie Davis, who sang most of the backing vocals, and offered many of the vocal arrangements. Valerie also became something of a mentor and friend to Love.

Apart from the originals, *Jennifer Love Hewitt* was interesting for its choice of covers. "I Want a Love I Can See" was an old Smokey Robinson song from the sixties that he'd performed with the Miracles, although it wasn't too well known. "I Was Always Your Girl" came from the catalogue of Everything But the Girl, dating from the late eighties.

Perhaps the strangest, though, was "(Our Love) Don't Throw It All Away," which had been a hit in the seventies for the late Andy Gibb.

Recording so quickly, during the breaks she had between her other work, was difficult for Love. There was no chance to concentrate and focus on her singing the way she needed. She still loved doing it, which made it all the more frustrating. And while R&B definitely suited her voice, it didn't completely reflect who she was; at home she was as likely to listen to alternative as anything else. But R&B also sold, that much was undeniable.

"Cool With You," the lead-off track from *Jennifer Love Hewitt*, was a sexy jam—but this was a very sexy album. Mid-tempo, it showcased Love's voice, which really caught the ear, more Toni Braxton than Mariah Carey this time out. It was proof that the girl who'd made *Let's Go Bang* was now really a woman, not just on the verge as she'd been before. But it was still romantic.

The same was true for the next cut, "No Ordinary Love," which was also the single. Mid-tempo, sultry, leaning to R&B but with enough pop in it to be catchy, it pretty much summed up the album. It was a song that should have been a hit, and with the right handling could have been, something that was also true of the album itself. Part of the problem, Love admitted, was her schedule.

"I just made [it] so fast, and I had no time to do any promotion so it just went nowhere."

Actually, with her name much better known through television, and now in movies, it did sell better than *Let's Go Bang*. But still the album sold nowhere near the amount it should have, even though "No Ordinary Love" did get a little airplay on *Party of Five*, during the second show of the season, in a scene with Julia, Claudia, and Claudia's boyfriend, Byron (Rider Strong).

Next came that Andy Gibb cover, which hadn't been totally Love's choice. Essentially, for this record, the producers had assembled the material, including the covers, and presented it to her. Some she loved, some she turned down—it was *her* album, after all—and this one made the cut, even though she wasn't familiar with it. Given a slow, simple arrangement, it made an effective, pleading ballad.

"Never a Day Goes By" appeared twice on the record, in the regular mix and an "acoustic version" which really wasn't too acoustic. It was a good song, but did it really warrant two appearances? That was hard to say. The second version definitely ventured into Mariah Carey territory—as close as this record came—with some lovely harmonies.

That mood stayed through "Don't Push the River," which just bubbled through the speakers. That was followed by the best track, "The Greatest Word," with a very soulful feel provided by some wah-wah guitar, the kind of thing that seemed to blend the sense of old Motown with modern R&B.

"I Want a Love I Can See," the Smokey Robinson cover, used chord changes similar to his famous "Tears of a Clown," and offered the best showcase for Love's voice, keeping the instruments in the background, and letting the vocals really carry the song, with lots of harmonies weaving around the lead.

From there it was into Everything But the Girl's "I Was Always Your Girl," from the period when they were a kind of high-class easy listening act. Again, the arrangement was low-key and very spare, with the voice just easing the tune out.

"Last Night" kicked in with a soft groove behind a swaying melody. About the only problem with it was that the song was generic, with little to make it very memorable.

That was certainly true when compared to the song

that followed it, the very different "I Believe In." This was as close to a rock song as the album proper came. Lyrically it was also different, talking about Anne Frank, teenage death, and the power of love to last through time. The interesting thing was that the song didn't sound out of place. It was soft rock, and somehow it seemed to capture Love's real vocal maturity. The guitars were played by Eric Bazilian, who'd once been a member of the Hooters (most memorable as the band that kicked off the Live Aid concert in 1985), and it wasn't a million miles from the type of material the Hooters had performed.

Apart from the "acoustic version" of "Never a Day Goes By" and Love's song from *House Arrest,* which had probably been added to help push the album to the people who'd seen the movie, that was it. She was proud of her work, and she had every reason to be. This was a considerable leap, stylistically, from her last effort.

She could have been accused of trying to cash in on her new-found television fame by releasing records, but that obviously wasn't the case. *Let's Go Bang* had been recorded before her first appearances on *Party of Five* ever aired. And though she'd sung on the show, performing a cover of Blondie's "Dreaming" with the Nielsens, this was definitely Jennifer Love Hewitt, not Sarah Reeves.

As with her last record, though, Atlantic didn't really push it, didn't try to get airplay for the songs. There was talk of a video, but if one was made, it was never shown anywhere. While the sales were far more encouraging than they'd been for *Let's Go Bang,* they still weren't earth-shattering. Mostly people bought the record because they'd heard about the disc from friends or on Web sites dedicated to *Party of Five* or to Love herself. After her first season on the show, Web sites dedicated to Love had begun to appear—all unofficial, of course. They were just the first wave; over the course of the next two years the numbers would grow and grow, until she was the fifth most accessed female star on the Internet.

Her fans were dedicated, and went out and bought *Jennifer Love Hewitt*. Not in enough numbers to make it a hit, but ample to warrant another record, although that would have to wait, and, in fact, is still waiting. When she does make another album, she's going to do it right, focus on it completely, and give it the time and energy it needs. But that's out of the question right now.

"I've kind of put music on the back burner for now," she explained, "because everything else is so busy, and I don't want to give it less than one hundred percent."

She hadn't stopped writing songs, although none of her compositions appeared on *Jennifer Love Hewitt*. And since she'd begun to learn the guitar, future records could possibly contain a number of her compositions, although the direction would probably be a little different. "[M]ore like Sarah MacLachlan or Jewel," she mused, which would certainly be a change from R&B.

Making a film and recording an album would be enough to fill anyone's free time. But not Jennifer. She had an offer to make another movie, to play one of the main characters—not the lead—and it was just too good to turn down. *Trojan War* (which was also known as *Rescue Me*) was a very well scripted, funny teen film, with some positive messages that it didn't try and push too fiercely.

More than that, its star would be someone she'd been thinking about from time to time: Will Friedle. Since their blind date, and Love's message on his intercom, he'd never called her. But that didn't mean he'd totally slipped out of her mind. She'd dated Joey Lawrence, although that was more or less over, since "business got in the way" as she diplomatically put it.

"The one thing I'll always be grateful for is that I

Jennifer at the Galaxy Theatre in Hollywood, CA.
(*Steve Granitz/Retna Limited, USA*)

At the Teen People Magazine Premiere Launch Party. (Jennifer was featured on the cover.)
(*Steve Granitz/Retna Limited, USA*)

Beautiful Jennifer in serious thought.
(Jay Blakesberg/Retna Limited, USA)

Hanging out for a night on the town at the Pangtages Theatre with Will Friedle in Hollywood, CA. (*Steve Granitz/Retna Limited, USA*)

Arriving at the Fourth Annual Blockbuster Entertainment Awards Show.
(*Steve Granitz/Retna Limited, USA*)

Jennifer strikes a playful pose.
(*Jon McKee/Retna Limited, USA*)

Jennifer and Melissa Joan Hart at the Teen People Magazine Premiere party.
(*Steve Granitz/Retna Limited, USA*)

Even in a quiet moment, Jennifer's star magnetism shines through.
(Jon McKee/Retna Limited, USA)

got to see a much different side of Joey than what people think, and if he called me and said he needed something, I'd be there in a heartbeat.''

It had been fun, but it wasn't the love thing by any means. With Will she felt . . . different, even if he didn't seem to feel the same way. He was making a name for himself as the star of *Boy Meets World,* and he was now testing the waters in movies. At twenty, he was three years older than Love, with a career that had run slightly longer than hers.

"I started acting in school when I was ten," he said. "I went into New York City and found a manager and the rest is history."

It was weird the way real life could be like fiction. While Love had her feelings for Will, there was something similar going on in *Trojan War.*

Brad (Will) was a senior, one week away from graduation. For twelve years he'd harbored a passion for the blond, blue-eyed Brooke, the loveliest girl in school, but a real dumb blonde. She, of course, had never noticed him, going instead for the football players as she became a cheerleader—the usual, predictable course. When they finished their year of biology, the teacher left a jar of condoms for the students. Brad didn't take one—he figured he'd have no use for it.

Brad was something of a nerd, who hung with his friends, including Leah (Love), the brainy tomboy who couldn't figure out what someone like Brad could see in a girl as vacuous as Brooke. It would probably have remained an unrequited passion, except for the fact that Brooke asked Brad over to tutor her in biology, so she could pass the course and graduate.

It was his dream come true, an entire evening with the object of his affection and lust. His friends envied him, except for Leah, who just found his obsession pathetic, even more so when he practiced his seduction lines on her.

Friday was the big evening, and Brad's father made it completely special by loaning Brad his pride and joy, a restored 1972 Jaguar XKE. But things didn't get off to a good start. He arrived at Brooke's only to find her boyfriend, Kyle, there. But she kicked Kyle out, and invited Brad into her bedroom to study.

After a little while it became apparent that Brooke was more interested in the practice of biology than the theory. The only problem was that Brad didn't have a condom. Running out of the house, he promised to be back in five minutes with the necessary protection.

And that was where everything went downhill.

He drove to the grocery store, where he bought candy, flowers, more candy, and condoms, then dashed out to the parking lot, only to discover that his father's very valuable car had been stolen.

That took him downtown, to report the theft to the police. Coming out of the precinct house, he tried to call Brooke, but the number she'd written on his hand (which he hadn't washed for four days), was no longer legible. Finally, he called Leah, and asked her to pick him up, arranging to catch a bus and meet her halfway.

Unfortunately, the phone had used all his money. He found himself the lone passenger on a bus (the same vehicle, incidentally, that had been used in *Speed*) with a psychotic driver who took him on a wild trip, dropping him . . . well, he had no idea where.

Brad walked around for a while, and eventually spotted a bar, which he entered in search of a phone. The problem was that he was the only gringo, and by far the smallest person in the room. Somehow or other he ended up being mistaken for *Baywatch*'s David Hasselhoff and winning $100 in a salsa contest, before escaping through the bathroom window.

Then he spotted what he believed was his dad's car speeding toward him. He stopped it, only to find it was now a lowrider, driven by three gangbangers—the ones who'd tagged his school the week before. When they learned that their artwork had been washed off, they headed back to the school, with Brad in tow. After asking him to finish their painting, they left Brad behind—taking the car with them.

All he wanted was a condom. And he spotted one, in the jar, in the biology lab. Breaking into the school, he took it. But he found himself confronted by a manic janitor who flushed him down the stairs with a fire hose, and came close to beating him up. Running away, he was pursued by his large salsa partner, before eventually finding Leah. She wanted to tell Brad how she really felt about him, but couldn't. Instead, she drove him back to Brooke's house.

His adventures were far from over. Soaked by the sprinklers, he discovered she wasn't answering the door. Attempting to climb in a window, he lost his condom, discovered a note saying Brooke had gone to a party, and found the house surrounded by police.

Brad did manage to make his escape, pursued by a German shepherd, only to end up at the country club where his parents were dancing the night away. With the dog after him, he stole a golf cart, and ended up in a Dumpster.

Buying clothes from a street person, he caught a bus to the party. First, though, he needed that condom. At the convenience store, with what little money he had left, he attempted to buy a pack, but it wasn't going to happen. Until the gangbangers he'd met earlier arrived to rob the place.

By the time they were leaving, the cops were outside, so they used a fairly willing Brad as a hostage to get away—in the XKE. A chase followed, the Jag got totaled, and Brad ended up back at the police station, where, finally, the cop gave him a condom.

He called his best friend, Leah, once more. But the Leah who picked him up this time was someone new and curvy, in a dress, looking like a girl. She'd been to the party herself.

Leah dropped Brad at the party, but found her car blocked in, unable to leave. Brad found Brooke, and they went upstairs. His dreams were all about to come true.

But they didn't. He realized that sex without love was nothing, or at least something he didn't want. He left, still a virgin, in pursuit of someone he did care about . . . Leah.

At first she didn't believe him, but a kiss managed to convince her. Things might just be okay.

For Love, too, it was a kiss that convinced her that she'd been right in thinking of Will as her "prince."

"When I kissed Will on-set, my knees felt weak. That had never happened to me before. After we finished the movie, I said to Will, 'So, are you ever gonna ask me out? I've been waiting . . . and I'm getting pretty sick of it.' So we went out for coffee and have been together since."

That alone made everything worthwhile for Love. She'd found the guy of her dreams, realized the two of them were right together long before he did, and finally convinced him that she was the one. *Trojan War* wasn't a movie that made it into the theaters—although it was as good as, and certainly funnier than, many that did. Instead, it went directly to video, not something a couple of young actors like Love and Will really wanted.

Of course, the movie was over the top and totally slapstick in places. But it was *meant* to be. And it displayed the right values of love over sex without ever being heavy-handed about it. What's more, even though the audience knew the story of Love and Will getting together by the time the video reached the stores, it was fun to see the chemistry between them onscreen, which was really obvious.

While it was Will's movie, Love easily stole pretty

much every scene she was in—she was more of a presence, and a better actor, than most of those around her.

She'd had a full summer already, and no real vacation, but it was far from over yet. Mostly because of Sarah on *Party of Five,* Jennifer had become a very recognizable person, one other girls looked up to as something of a role model. And the real girl wasn't that different, either. She'd achieved so much, not only with her acting, but also with her music.

That was why Sears and *Seventeen* magazine asked her to spend a couple of weeks touring on their behalf, going to malls in six different cities around the country, and speaking to people. There'd be question-and-answer sessions; and Love would get to sing some songs from her new record, offer some advice, and sign a few autographs—well, a lot of autographs, actually. She was to be the spokesperson for the second annual Peak Performance contest, which was co-sponsored by *Seventeen* and Sears business centers. The winners of the contest—all girls between the ages of thirteen and twenty-one—would receive academic scholarships.

She was honored by the request, she said. It meant a great deal to her.

"I had a lot of fun going around to different malls in cities and talking to girls and performing songs from my album. It was a lot of fun and will always be a huge honor for me."

Obviously, because of her schedule, there was a limit as to just how much she could do, but it did give her a chance to get outside L.A. and see what people thought of her, and the show, in other parts of the United States.

Mall appearances weren't anything new; in the eighties Tiffany had used them to launch a career that turned her into a singing star, and in their early days the Backstreet Boys had played malls and high schools, anywhere that would have them. But it wasn't often that an established teen star (which was what Love had become) toured malls.

As a regular girl, Jennifer Love was familiar with mall culture, and the part it played in the life of teens (including herself).

She'd traveled virtually all over the world before, when she was younger, but this was the first time Love had toured her native land. She got to find out just how many fans *Party of Five* had all over America. Crowds of people came out to see her; the response was overwhelming. So overwhelming, that a singing date was booked for her in Los Angeles for that November 3, performing at the House of Blues on Sunset Boulevard.

And then, without a break, it was time to go and do some real work again.

Chapter Eight

The third season of *Party of Five* (and Love's second season with the show) would see much more happening, and Sarah would be involved in a great deal of it. She would have a distant brush with death herself, and face some major problems with Bailey.

The season would also begin early, with the first episode aired in August 1996 (September, or even October, was when the new seasons for shows traditionally began). It meant that the show would start out with fresh episodes playing against summer reruns on other channels, in the hope that new viewers would tune in.

Party of Five had fully established its identity by now, and found its core audience in the 18-to-34 age demographic. What it needed to do was expand on that base, which was precisely what FOX wanted to do. So, in February 1997, they teamed with Dr Pepper and Express clothing stores in a $15 million ad campaign, the largest the network had ever undertaken, to bring the show to the masses. There were ads everywhere, in magazines, newspapers, on television, and competitions with prizes like *Party of Five* merchandise and trips to Hollywood.

It seemed to work. Over the course of the year, more and more people discovered the show and became hooked on it, tuning in week after week. By the end of the season, *Party of Five* had risen to number eighty-three overall on the Nielsen ratings. That still didn't make it a smash hit like *ER* or *Friends,* but it was well out of the basement where it had originally languished, and it was now positioned in the higher bracket of FOX shows—no mean feat for a show that had come very close to cancellation just a couple of years before.

What helped it was the combination of excellent acting, great scripts, and some very strong, realistic storylines. But other, attendant publicity didn't hurt, either, and much of that came from Neve Campbell. In the hiatus between the second and third seasons, she'd starred in *Scream,* a horror film from the pen of Kevin Williamson, who'd go on to write *I Know What You Did Last Summer* and the television series *Dawson's Creek.* No one had very high hopes for the movie, but it struck a chord with teens, and became a huge hit at the box office, ending up as one of the major money-making films of the year. Neve became a full-fledged star, hosting *Saturday Night Live* and forging a movie career, and that shone the spotlight more brightly on the show.

Love too would spread her television wings during the season. The popularity of Sarah led MTV to ask her to host a special called "True Tales of Teen Trauma," because she was a teen who attracted viewers, one they could relate to. And she joined some other big names from the FOX network to host a Halloween special, an event she'd long remember—for all the wrong reasons.

"I was performing in Florida, for the FOX Halloween bash, and I realized that I did my entire performance with a hole in the crotch area of my pants!"

The amazing thing was that no one said anything, although millions of people saw it. Love said, once she realized, that "it was kind of humiliating."

Sarah's season got under way in the very first episode, when she joined Bailey and Will's road trip down to Mexico. Bailey had hoped it would be guys only, but

Will invited Sarah and his girlfriend, Gina (Alanna Ubach) to join them. Bailey's idea had been to have a wild time south of the border, which wasn't exactly the kind of sightseeing the girls had in mind—meaning that nothing was going to go as originally planned. And things became even worse when Bailey's Jeep was stolen. Bailey's underlying anger throughout the trip, though, had little to do with Sarah, or even the change in itinerary, but more with the fact that Will was going away to college, while Bailey would be staying in San Francisco, surrounded by family, for his schooling.

He would change that, however. While almost everyone he knew was moving out of town, at least he could move out of the Salinger house. He went out and found a house to share with a young couple.

In the meantime, by pure coincidence, a link was forged with another show. Love was now definitely involved with *Boy Meets World*'s Will Friedle. One of his co-stars on the show, Rider Strong, began guesting on *Party of Five* as Byron, the new boyfriend Claudia had acquired at camp.

Sarah was none too happy with Bailey's new living arrangements. She liked Bailey at home, where he was under control, and where he had really been the surrogate parent of the family, looking after everybody. But he was maturing, he needed to spread his wings a little. She became truly upset, though, when one member of the couple—the man—moved out of the house, leaving Bailey living alone with the woman, Callie Martel (Alexondra Lee), whom Sarah categorized as "a nubile exhibitionist." Sarah sensed danger, but Bailey tried to reassure her, promising that, as long as he and Sarah were together, he would never be attracted to another woman.

Callie proved to be more than a handful for Bailey. She invented stories about a stalker, and he believed her, having no reason not to, even when she claimed that the stalker was one of Bailey's college professors, which proved to be a complete lie. Still, for some reason—probably just because he was Bailey—he continued to stay in the house with her, rather than move home again.

And that would prove to be his undoing. Bailey wanted to be adult, to live his own life. Which didn't include revisiting high school for a Halloween dance with Sarah. He'd left high school now, and the idea of going back for a senior dance, with the two of them dressed as Prince Charming and Sleeping Beauty, just seemed juvenile. They argued about it, and Bailey decided to drown his sorrows, and his anger, in beer. For the first time, alcohol would be his downfall. Drunk, and not used to it, he ended up sleeping with his roommate.

Being Bailey, he couldn't do anything without anguish, and the next day he was regretting everything. The only fair thing to do, he decided, was to break up with Sarah. He felt as if the guilt were written all over his face . . . but he was wrong. Instead, it was chicken pox, and his illness enabled him to see Callie's true colors. She didn't want to deal with him when he was sick. Instead, it was Sarah who brought over the chicken soup, and did everything she could to make him comfortable. That alone was enough to make him think twice about breaking up with her.

However he looked at it, though, Callie was his roommate, and that meant he owed her something. When a date tried to rape her, it was a recovered Bailey who saved her. The problem with Callie was that she needed a man around—and she was beginning to discover that Bailey was handy. That didn't do Sarah much good, though. She even tried to make friends with Callie, but Callie wasn't the type to befriend other women—at least, not when there was a man around.

The next two episodes marked a real turning point in the relationship between Sarah and Bailey. She tried to set Callie up with her cousin Paul (Don Jeffcoat), but

Callie insisted on a double date—and Sarah couldn't seem to get Bailey to herself. When she did, and he wanted to finally make love to her, he found himself unable to perform, leaving himself depressed and Sarah saddened at the way everything was going. However, a few hours later, back at his apartment, he had no trouble "performing" with Callie after he'd gotten drunk.

Now he felt doubly guilty, and he did the only thing he could—he told Sarah the truth about his infidelities. Of course it was devastating for her. She loved him, and the idea of being with anyone else would never enter her head. It seemed as if she'd break up with him forever, but Sarah simply realized she loved Bailey too much to let him go.

Callie was definitely the bad girl, and Alexondra Lee, who played her, knew it.

"Everyone loves Love and I come in and break them up!" she told *Sassy* gleefully.

But she hadn't... not yet. Bailey was depressed. Sarah had gone away for the Christmas holiday, and so had Callie, leaving him all alone with his guilt in the apartment... until Christmas Day, when he finally showed up at the Salinger house. That merriment was just a temporary reprieve. When Sarah returned, she and Bailey found they were just sniping at each other. He felt as if he couldn't meet her standards, and she simply couldn't let go of the fact that he'd cheated on her. If she stayed with him, they'd just continue to fight, and Sarah would hate herself for not having any self-respect. She did the only thing she could—she broke up with Bailey.

That was the catalyst for one of the season's ongoing storylines—Bailey's alcoholism. After he and Sarah broke up, he began losing himself in drink. When Claudia wanted to go out with him and celebrate after he won his All-State wrestling qualifiers, he went out drinking instead, using his fake ID to get into bars. His low academic performance due to drinking forced him to drop a class.

When Will came home from college for a visit he was astonished at the way Bailey was drinking. Bailey, of course, shrugged it all off, staying in denial. Will even tried to enlist Sarah's help, but it was too soon; she needed time to distance herself from Bailey before she could be his friend and help him.

Sarah, however, could tell Julia, and that was exactly what she did. At first Julia didn't want to believe her friend, but slowly she came to understand that Bailey was an alcoholic. That became even more apparent when he had to hire a clown for little Owen's birthday party. Instead, the money was spent on booze, and a drunken Bailey in a clown suit turned up and ruined the party. At that point even Charlie was willing to believe what Sarah and Julia had been telling him about his brother.

The family—and that included Sarah, who was still probably closer to him than anyone—had to do something. On a ruse they got him over to the Salinger house, where they all confronted him. He responded in the typical manner of the alcoholic, insulting everybody. But Bailey was forced to shut up when Joe (Tom Mason) arrived and told Bailey that his father had been an alcoholic, albeit a recovered one.

At that point, for the first time, Bailey admitted he had a problem. Still, though, he stormed away from his family.

He had a long way to go, however. He picked up Owen from preschool, and kept him out all night, panicking the entire family. When he finally brought the child home, Bailey was drunk. The only person who might be able to reach him was Sarah, and she took off after him, trying to persuade him that he was in no fit condition to drive.

He, of course, took off with her in the Jeep, and the worst happened; Bailey's erratic driving got them into an accident, and while Bailey didn't even have a scratch, Sarah ended up in the hospital. She only had a concussion and some lacerations, but for a while it looked worse.

That marked the turning point for Bailey. They might not be dating, but he loved Sarah, and couldn't bear the thought that he might have seriously injured her, or even killed her. When she came to in her hospital bed, Bailey was there, crying and asking for her help to quit drinking.

Having taken the first big step, he decided to attend AA. But at his first meeting, he saw the driver who'd killed his parents. That was enough to turn him off. He announced to his family that he was going to tough it out alone, without the help of any organization. Long-suffering Sarah offered to help him through it all, being a good friend—and still more than a little in love with Bailey.

And he, of course, was still in love with her. A part of him had hoped that they might get back together once he quit drinking, but she let him know that wasn't going to happen anytime soon. She'd be his friend, his crutch when he needed one, but not his girlfriend again. To emphasize the point, she began dating Drew (Christopher Gartin) from her doctor's office, leaving Bailey jealous, and realizing just how much he cared for Sarah.

Quitting drinking was more than just a case of stopping, however. Staying stopped was much harder, as Bailey discovered when he accompanied Claudia to Los Angeles for a rehearsal. He'd wanted to prove himself as responsible, and reluctantly the family had given him the chance. Their worst fears came true when he drank the entire minibar in the hotel. It took Joe to point out to Bailey that though he might have inherited his father's problem with alcohol, he'd also inherited the strength that had made his father stop drinking. With that food for thought, back in San Francisco, Bailey began attending AA meetings again.

He hadn't stopped believing that he and Sarah could get back together, though, and when they kissed, he was certain it was going to happen. The mature one, Sarah, with her feet firmly planted on the ground, had to sit him down and explain everything. They had a history. Things had once been perfect, but they'd come a long way since then, and no matter what happened, it was impossible to go back to the way it had once been. She cared very deeply about Bailey, and wanted to be around him, but the only way she could do it was as his friend. He had to accept that.

And he did, reluctantly. Better to have Sarah by him in some capacity than not at all. At least, if she was still a part of his life, the possibility of winning her back existed.

After half a season of "would they, wouldn't they get back together," had the new relationship between Sarah and Bailey been defined? As the third season of the show ended, it appeared that way. But this was *Party of Five*. For a while it had even seemed possible they might wed, as promotional spots for the show had dropped hints of *someone* getting married; in the event, that was Julia and Griffin. But there was enough ambiguity, and real love, in Sarah and Bailey's relationship that anything could—and probably would—happen in the future. Leaving it like that had the viewers hooked. And not only the viewers. Even the cast had no idea what lay ahead. All Love could offer was that "Sarah will definitely be back as strong as ever. But actually, right now, I have no idea what will be happening in future episodes." She did, however, drop a few hints for the 1997–98 season: "Bailey and Sarah, as far as I know, are in for a season of very exciting events. But it wouldn't be any fun to watch if we all knew what was going to happen." And elsewhere she added, "It's hard to tell if Sarah and Bailey are going to get back together right now. I know Scott and I aren't sure. I don't think the writers are sure if we're going to get back together. You just have to keep watching and see."

She was especially pleased with the way the entire Sarah and Bailey situation had been handled over the course of the season.

"I think that the relationship between Bailey and Sarah is very much like a real relationship," she said. "I think all the relationships on *Party of Five* are pretty real and accurate on the way things happen."

There'd been plenty on the show to make her think about love and life. If a boyfriend had hurt her in an accident while driving drunk, she had to admit that she wasn't certain what her own reaction would be.

"I don't think I can answer that question without having been put in that position. But I have to say that if you fall in love, it's amazing what you'd put up with and what you'd take."

She certainly understood the feelings that Sarah and Bailey had for each other.

"[T]hey are two characters on TV who are really in love, even though they're not together. Although they are not boyfriend and girlfriend, they really care for each other. That's not too common on TV, and Bailey and Sarah are two people who genuinely care for each other."

Love was also very happy with the way her character had grown over the course of the two seasons she'd been on *Party of Five,* and the direction Sarah's relationship with Bailey had taken.

"I think she's a strong independent young woman who has a lot going for her. I think she and Bailey are dependent on each other because they have something that they each need. They look at each other with no judgment, and they're the only two people that they found that way."

She was also pleased with the way *Party of Five* had

dealt with Bailey's alcoholism, which was, after all, a relatively major teen issue.

"I thought the way the show handled it was very graceful and strong. I hope in some small way we were able to either stop people from becoming addicted or show those who already have a problem that they should get help." And the way to do that, of course, was not to preach, but rather illuminate just how bad things could be, to be as realistic about it as the show had been with other issues it had faced.

The end of *Party of Five*'s third season was important for Jennifer Love Hewitt in a couple of ways. In February of 1997, she'd turned eighteen, and officially become an adult.

"Before I was eighteen, I was constantly frustrated when my ten-and-a-half-hour workday was up on the set, because I wasn't tired and I didn't want to go home. But they couldn't let me stay, because my hours were limited under California labor laws." After that milestone, she was able to work the same twelve-to-fourteen-hour days as the rest of the cast.

It also marked another important turning point— Love graduated from high school. Although she'd been tutored on sets for most of the time she'd been in California, her work was assessed through a regular high school. That meant she'd be graduating with that class, although she'd never been there, and didn't know anyone. To make it all the more stressful, *People* came and covered her graduation ceremony.

"It didn't bother me," she recalled. "The crew was very nice, but I was worried about what the other kids might think. I just kind of went along with it, but I would have rather they hadn't been there."

However, it was an indication of just how much of a celebrity she'd become that the magazine found such a story newsworthy.

People readers weren't the only ones who found it

interesting. Love's graduation brought an encounter of sorts with her screen heartthrob, Johnny Depp. She'd loved him in *Don Juan DeMarco*, her favorite movie of all time, so much so that she named one of her cats Don Juan. She'd never really expected to have anything to do with the man himself, however. That came about by coincidence.

Love had a regular driver to take her to and from home to the *Party of Five* set.

"My driver was going to the airport to pick up Johnny Depp," Love told *Teen People*. "I asked him to say hello for me, and he did. He also told Johnny I was going to be graduating. The next thing I know, there's a message on my answering machine saying, 'My brother wants to send you flowers. Please call with your address.' I called and asked, 'Who's your brother?' She said, 'Johnny Depp.' I was like, 'Excuse me?'"

And, as good as his word, Depp did send a large basket of wildflowers to celebrate Love's graduation. Far more important to someone with a major Johnny Depp obsession, he enclosed a card, which said, "I know how hard it is in this business to do what you did. Congratulations, I'm very proud of you. All my love, Johnny."

In fact, that actually led to her eventually meeting him, one of the biggest thrills of her life. One of the lighting crew on *Party of Five* knew Depp, and knew just how much of a fan Love was. He arranged for Depp to visit and meet the girl who'd received his flowers—all as a surprise.

"It was one of those days when you just show up in your sweats and no makeup and I just looked hideous. So I'm in my trailer when the makeup girl goes, 'Johnny Depp is standing right outside.' I looked outside and sure enough he was there. I threw myself on my trailer floor screaming hysterically, 'I can't meet him! I can't meet him!' So I ran right out, right past him—screaming—and I locked myself in the makeup trailer.''

Of course, that was the end of that—almost. As soon as she thought about it, Love felt stupid. Here was someone she'd really wanted to meet, someone who'd come to the set specifically to meet her, and she'd acted like a kid.

She did have a chance to make amends a couple of months later. She was sent tickets for the premiere of Depp's new movie, *Donnie Brasco,* and waited so long outside the theater to get a glimpse of him that her seat was given away. When he finally arrived, Love yelled his name, he turned and waved. She absolutely *had* to meet him, and went on to the place where the premiere party would be held after the showing. After some explanation and some sweet talk, the security guard let her in, and she finally did get to meet her hero, who said, ''Thanks for all the sweet things you've said about me.''

That would have been enough to have made her content for the rest of her life, but there was a postscript. A little while later, Depp called her when she was on the set, to see how she was, and also to invite her for coffee the next time she was in New York. It was the fulfillment of every dream she'd ever had about a star.

Now, with the season over, there was time for Jennifer Love to take a vacation. At least, the *time* was there, but not the inclination. The year before, Neve Campbell had made *Scream,* which had done so well. Now Love was following in her footsteps down the winding path of horror, having signed to star in her first feature. She was over eighteen now, and so she felt she was ready for that. It was a film written by Kevin Williamson, who'd also penned *Scream,* called *I Know What You Did Last Summer.*

Chapter Nine

Horror definitely wasn't Love's genre. For viewing she preferred comedy or romance, "but once I found out I was going to be in one, I watched, like, four of them, including *The Shining*. I was terrified—I couldn't sleep for days. But I wanted to get myself used to things I was going to see on the set."

The others she rented were *Nightmare on Elm Street* ("not only because it was scary, but because Johnny Depp was in it!"), *The Omen, Scream,* and *In the Mouth of Madness*. Seeing them might have given her sleepless nights, but they did help her prepare for the role of Julie James. "[T]hrowing myself into the middle of one [genre] kind of helped me overcome my biggest fear. Now I can have a little more fun with them."

Someone who was definitely able to offer some help was Neve Campbell, who'd already had experience with all this.

"We had, like, this really Hollywood moment where she and I were sitting on the steps in the Salingers' house on the set. And she was reading a script, and I was reading the script for *I Know What You Did Last Summer*. And she kinda goes, 'Oh, what are you reading?' I'm like, 'I'm reading this thing. It's written by Kevin Williamson.' And I was like, 'Oh, you know Kevin.' She's like, 'Yeah, I do. I think the world of him.' And she goes, 'Is it, like, a horror film?' And I said, 'Yeah.' All she said is, 'If you have the chance to do it—if you get the part—you absolutely have to. You will never have as much fun in your entire life. You'll also never be as tired, but you will never have as much fun as you'll have when you do a horror film.' And so that kinda stuck at the back of my mind, and when I got the chance to do the movie, I was like, 'Neve said it was going to be a lot of fun, so...' She was right. She was definitely right."

Her co-stars on the project would be Freddie Prinze, Jr., son of the late actor Freddie Prinze, and Sarah Michelle Gellar, who was much better known to television audiences as Buffy in the series *Buffy the Vampire Slayer*.

"I got *Last Summer* the same week that *Buffy* premiered," Gellar explained. "I went to North Carolina to film the movie, and *Buffy* wasn't televised in the small town where we were shooting," Gellar explained. "I was spared from it right away, while all this craze was happening."

Cast and crew set up in Southport, North Carolina (the location home for a new TV series called *Dawson's Creek*, also penned by Kevin Williamson, which actually began shooting while *I Know* was filming), which was well away from the frantic pace of L.A. It seemed like the ideal place, somewhat isolated and picturesque. But the locals weren't as receptive as everyone had hoped. They didn't want to be invaded by Hollywood types, and, according to Gellar, "They would close restaurants down when they saw us coming."

For Love, though, it was one of the best experiences of her life, particularly working with director Jim Gillespie.

"He's by far the best director I've ever worked with. He was *amazing* with our crew, we worked seventeen-hour days. He never got frustrated and never yelled at the crew, he was always right there to tell us what an amazing job we'd done."

She was also very happy that she was able to help shape her character.

"Jim and I had a conversation in regards to Julie. We took her to say, 'I'm going to cry later... break down, later on. I'm going to be strong now and my human instincts are going to help me survive and I'm going to try and beat the bloody pulp out of this guy if he comes anywhere near me.'" In other words, she wasn't just going to be a weak stereotype. "It's better to show that, just because you're afraid of something, it doesn't mean the female has to curl up into a ball and cry in the corner and the male has to step in and do everything. Jim wanted Julie to be very strong. He wanted her to kick some major butt, whether the guy's around or not. My favorite thing in the movie is that she took care of business."

And indeed she did. But while the movie might have been horror, the set was anything but. Just like on the set of *Party of Five*, when some darker, more emotional subject matter was part of the script, everybody liked to clown around and have a lot of fun to relieve all the tension.

"[W]e did a take, just for dailies, where I see a dead body and scream. And then I reached over, and gave the corpse a big kiss on the cheek, and said, 'You are so beautiful.' There were lots of moments when it got really late at night, like when we were on a boat and we started singing 'Rock the Boat, Baby.' You'd hear us at four in the morning. It was like, 'Are we filming *Grease*?' with spectators going, 'What is going on here?'"

Of course, it could also get a little weird for everyone, and Love was no exception.

"I thought I was seeing crazy fishermen everywhere, like the one who pursues us in the film... One night, on the way home from the set, I see this fisherman standing on the side of the road in his slicker—just standing there in the dark. And I'm like, 'Oh my God, go a little faster.' The next morning, we were driving back, and I look, and he's still just standing there. Then I realized it was a cardboard fisherman: a *sign* advertising some fish restaurant. That's the way the filming affected my psyche. Everyone thought I was a little nuts."

One thing she did realize, though, was that you couldn't fake a scream—not that she had to, really, with her feelings about horror movies.

"You've just got to go full out," Love explained. "If you lose your voice, you lose it, and you just have to wait for it to come back . . . [T]he second day of filming I had to do two screaming scenes and two yelling scenes. The third day, I came in, and I'd lost my voice. So the director added more extras in the background, and turned it into a whispering scene, as if I was trying to be very quiet."

Probably the most obviously noticeable thing about Love in this movie was that her outfits featured some serious cleavage. She and director Gillespie had discussed this beforehand, and he'd pointed out to her that teenage boys really preferred to see girls who had at least some glamour and some flesh.

"I think that especially in the entertainment industry it is a known fact that no one is going to watch a movie that stars a girl with no makeup, pimples on her face, greasy hair, and sweat," Love explained. "It's just not going to happen. They need eye candy. They need something to be watching when the scenes that they're not getting something from are going on. They need something visual to draw them into the theater to see that. So, if my outfit in *I Know What You Did Last Summer* helped with that, if it did that, great. That's fine . . . I don't mind being eye candy. It's incredibly flattering, because I don't look at myself that way, so it's, like, 'Great. You think I'm something to look at. Cool.' That's fine. I don't mind that stuff at all. I'll never do the nude scenes; that's just totally unnecessary and ridiculous, but I'll wear the outfits, and I'll feed into the eye-candy thing as much as I can without going over a certain line."

If anything, the boob factor in the film made everyone involved laugh.

"There was a joke on the set about how we were going to have to rename the movie *I Know What Your Breasts Did Last Summer,* because there was a pair of them flying around on every scene in the movie—it was either mine or Sarah's. When I saw the movie I had to go home and look in the mirror again and go, 'Maaan! What is going on?' "

Amazingly, Love didn't—and still doesn't—consider herself a total babe, but just an ordinary person.

"We all have days when we look at ourselves and go, 'I look pretty darned good today,' but I think of myself as pretty average," she said. "You can't be an actress and not be concerned about how you look, but I'm glad I don't focus on it that much ... If everybody looked the same—perfect, beautiful, clear skin—it would be boring. You can play around, try new, exciting things—makeup, a new hairstyle—but you can't really change how you look—it makes you who you are."

Of course, she also worked out regularly with a personal trainer to stay in shape. Not just for looks and the bod, but also for the energy to get through a shoot—the filming of *I Know What You Did Last Summer* took ten weeks—or the grind of being in a series, week in and week out. She was the kind of girl who could go from queen to tomboy like that in real life.

"I love that whole princess mentality, but I also like throwing my hair in a ponytail and just wearing jeans, going on a hike and then eating a big chili cheeseburger."

She needed to be in shape for the movie, since she'd elected to do most of her own stunt work, something she hadn't really thought about. It proved more grueling than she'd imagined, and Love was a frequent visitor to the set nurse for bruises (she ended up with a total of thirty-eight) and lacerations, as well as a scratch on her eye when she fell on a piece of rusty metal. Nothing major, but enough to give her plenty of aches.

Perhaps the biggest problem with filming was that, since it was taking place on the East Coast, it kept her away from Will. They were still going strong, but they hardly had any time together, given the busy schedules they both had. Of course, in some ways that did help, since the time they could share became even more special. If they needed a little privacy, they could always go to his apartment across the street from Love's since he lived alone. And there was always the McDonald's date, giving them both a chance to exercise their passion for junk food. That meant specifically a McDonald's #2 Value Meal, supersized. That way they each got a cheeseburger, they could share the Coke, and Love was able to eat all the fries.

Certainly she deserved them after seventy days of filming that kept her apart from Will. And she deserved them even more when the film opened in October 1997.

Based on Lois Duncan's novel, *I Know What You Did Last Summer* was set around successive Fourth of Julys. Julie James (Love) and Helen Shivers (Sarah Michelle Gellar) were best friends who'd just graduated high school in Southport, North Carolina, a small fishing community. Julie was the brain, who'd be leaving on a scholarship to attend college in Boston. Helen was the bod, who'd just won the local beauty pageant, and had plans to move to New York and become an actress. After the pageant they took off with their boyfriends for the beach. Helen was dating the rich kid, Barry Cox (Ryan Phillippe), a complete jerk, while Julie was with the more sensitive Ray Bronson (Freddie Prinze, Jr.).

Barry was too drunk to drive home, so Ray took his keys and handled the BMW. He was distracted when Barry dropped his booze, however, and hit something. It turned out they'd killed—or almost killed—a fisherman. Barry was mostly upset about the damage to his car. The others wanted to go to the police, but he wouldn't let them. Instead, they stashed the body in the trunk, took it to the deserted harbor, and tipped it in the water, with vows never to mention the incident again. Just as they were pushing it off the dock, though, the body came briefly to life. No longer was this an accident. Now it was murder. Or so it seemed.

One year later, Julie returned to Southport. At the end of the college year she'd stayed for summer school, in an attempt to raise her grades, because she'd been bombing out badly. A note awaited her. No postmark, no return address. It said simply, "I know what you did last summer."

Julie decided to find the others. Going to Shivers' Department Store, she asked Elissa, Helen's sister, for Helen's New York number. There was no need. Helen was right there. New York had been a washout. Julie had had no contact with the others since the previous summer. In fact, none of them had had contact since then. Julie and Helen went to see Barry, and they discovered that he was still a drunk and a jerk. Ray too hadn't left town; he was working on a fishing boat.

Their fears became real when the BMW was stolen, and used to run him down, but not kill him. He had seen the driver—a man in a fisherman's slicker, holding a hook.

Julie, the one who felt most guilty, had already discovered that the person she thought they'd killed was a man called David Egan, whose fiancée had died the year before his death, and she decided these threats must involve some friend of his. She and Helen went to his house, where they discovered his sister Missy (Anne Heche), a rather dislocated young woman.

They knew the killer was out there, but they had no idea who it was. The morning of July 4, Julie got a call from a terrified Helen. In the night someone had come into her room and cut her hair—just as she was due to appear in the parade and pageant as the outgoing queen. Julie drove over, but heard a strange noise from the trunk. Pulling over and opening it, she discovered the body of Max, a schoolfriend who'd driven by the four on that fateful night a year before.

When she, Helen, and Barry returned to the car, the body was gone, of course. But life was getting seriously weird. Helen took part in the parade, and saw the fisherman, hidden in his slicker and sou'wester. But Barry, her knight in shining armor, had gone after someone else. At the pageant, Barry stood in the balcony, to protect her. And that was where the fisherman got him. Helen saw it, ran screaming from the stage, but when she and a cop checked the balcony, they found nothing.

The cop took her home, but was forced to stop on the way to help a stranded motorist. It was the fisherman, who gutted him with the hook, then took off after Helen, chasing her to the family department store, where her sister Elsa was stocktaking. He killed her, and eventually caught up with Helen in an alley, just yards from the big holiday parade.

Julie, meanwhile, had been doing some research. She'd seen a tattoo that read "Susie" (the name of David's dead fiancée) on the person they'd killed, and Missy had told her that her brother never had a tattoo. Missy had mentioned a friend, a "Billy Blue" visiting, but there was no record of anyone by that name. However, she wondered if the fisherman could be Susie's father, Benjamin Willis. She found Ray on the dock, but ran when she saw the name of his boat: *Billy Blue*.

A man knocked Ray out as he followed her, and guided her to his boat for safety.

Once she was on board, he cast off, and Julie realized she was face-to-face with the fisherman. There was no escape. Ray took a skiff and followed them, climbing on board. Willis was pursuing Julie as she ran into the ice room, where she uncovered the bodies of Barry and Helen. Willis knocked Ray overboard again, but he climbed back, catching Willis with some heavy equipment as he was going for Julie.

Julie and Ray seemed safe—until Willis regained consciousness. But when he went after them, his hook caught in some netting. Ray hit a lever, and Willis went up, his hand (with hook) severed, and his body was thrown into the water.

The adventure was over. They could get on with their lives. And Ray and Julie could become a couple again.

The next summer, Julie was at school. She'd made the dean's list, and was preparing to go home, about to take a shower. A note, with no address, suddenly terrified her—but it was just an invitation to a party. Then in the condensation on the glass outside the shower room, she saw the words "I Still Know," as the glass shattered.

The scene was handily set for a sequel.

As he had with *Scream* (and would with *Scream 2*), Kevin Williamson had created a fast-paced script, with teenage characters who were very real, not the cardboard cutouts of so many horror flicks. He'd also made the girls very strong, not the helpless, whimpering victims so common in the genre. Julie used her brain and her computer to figure out who the fisherman probably was. Helen at least fought back. And Williamson put plenty of humor into the screenplay, with lots of sly references and jokes. When Helen originally outlined her career plans for Barry, she was going to become a regular on the TV soap, *Guiding Light*. Sarah Michelle

Gellar herself had spent two years on a daytime soap, *All My Children*, and had in fact won a daytime Emmy for her work. And when Julie and Ray decided to get very close on the beach, the camera cut to scenes of waves on the shore, a clear reference to the fifties film *From Here to Eternity*.

To be fair, there were things that made absolutely no sense—but they did keep viewers' eyes focused on the screen, as did Jennifer's and Sarah's cleavage factor, without ever being intrusive.

Whatever the reason, the film worked in a very big way. Once it was released, it took off like a rocket, following strongly in the footsteps of *Scream*, whose success had taken everyone by surprise. Most people assumed that the age of the teen slasher movie had passed, but an intelligent, well-written, funny slasher movie was something new. *Scream* proved that, and so did *I Know What You Did Last Summer*, which took in more than $71 million at the box office.

People felt that it was "fine for what it is but is neither slick enough nor terrifying enough to convert non-horror fans," and added that "TV babes Hewitt and Sarah Michelle Gellar add what depth they can to their roles and run like hell when the hook appears." *Variety* agreed that "the leads elevate their prototypes considerably, leaping over seemingly impossible dialogue to convey vulnerability and burdensome guilt. Hewitt and Prinze are particularly good," and went on to say that the movie was "just clever enough to rise above the usual fodder, [and] its appealing cast and technical confidence go a long way toward paving over narrative and character lapses."

It was exactly what it was meant to be—one hundred minutes of relatively mindless entertainment. It didn't have pretensions to be high art or superior drama. It was a great date movie, something to watch, laugh at, and be terrified by. Did it need to be more than that?

Certainly audiences didn't think so. They put down their money to see it once, twice, several times, which said far more than any reviewer ever could.

"I was utterly and completely shocked," Love said. "I knew it was going to be a good movie, but I didn't know that so many other people would get into it. I was incredibly shocked."

Most importantly, it made a real star of Jennifer Love Hewitt. Before *I Know* she'd been slowly carving out a career for herself. After she joined *Party of Five, Entertainment Weekly* welcomed her to the cast, saying "the best thing about the short-lived *Shaky Ground, Byrds of Paradise,* and *McKenna* has found a home as Sarah, Bailey's latest flame."

Sarah was how she'd become known, but the success of *I Know* put her in a completely different league. Not only with fans, but also within the industry, which realized something was going on. There had been a sudden surge in teen stars, not just in music, where they'd always been evident, but in television and in the movies. Instead of going for the big, familiar names, teen audiences were making stars out of people their own age, and out of shows that reflected their own lives. Things hadn't been like this in a long time, but teens themselves hadn't really been like this, either. They had money, and in large part because of the Internet, they had power. Having grown up with computers, they were using them to contribute heavily to newsgroups, and also to build Web sites that reflected their interests, in shows and in actors. And those Web sites were scoring heavy hits each and every day. Teens were going in droves to see movies like *Scream* and *I Know What You Did Last Summer*. The young actors and directors too understood that something was going on. Instead of seeing themselves as just taking part in a schlock exercise, they realized that they were the future, they could be taken seriously.

As Love pointed out, in the eighties, there were the John Hughes teen movies (which she loved), most of which seemed to star Molly Ringwald. But more recently, people like Claire Danes and Leonardo DiCaprio had become major stars, due in large part to teen audiences. They were bankable, and they were carrying movies.

"I think because of that we have more teenage actors that are believing in themselves, that are coming forward going, 'I'm the next Harrison Ford, I'm the next Jodie Foster,' whatever. And so there's amazing talent, as far as the younger generation of actors goes . . ."

Of course, she was at the forefront of that. Not the next Jodie Foster, but the first, and only, Jennifer Love Hewitt. And that would be enough to take her many places.

Certainly, she was beginning to get some recognition. In 1997 the *Hollywood Reporter* named her Best Young Star, for her work on *Party of Five*, and that was quickly followed by the 1998 Blockbuster Entertainment Award for Favorite Female Newcomer. *GQ* listed her as a "slammin' babe"—when she read it "I was screaming in my house." There was absolutely no doubt about it, Love was going places.

Chapter Ten

After a horror-filled summer, albeit one that was also a lot of fun, Love was more than ready for the relative sanity of a new season of *Party of Five*.

But although the cast would have fun, it was going to be a heavily dramatic season for the show, enough to make the first three seem like a light-hearted romp in the woods. Possibly even *too* dramatic—the show would take a brief hiatus late in the season and return with episodes that were much happier.

The biggest storyline would be Charlie's ongoing battle with cancer (Hodgkin's disease), but that was only the first problem for the Salingers. Julia would have to deal with her husband's infidelity. Claudia, unable to handle everything happening at home, would become a truant from school, which in turn would lead to her and Owen being taken into care briefly.

"This season, for the first time in a long time, the family unit as a whole was threatened," explained co-creator Amy Lippman.

Above all, it was a successful season for *Party of Five*, with ratings twenty-three percent above the previous year, enough to guarantee its renewal.

"It's not often that you have something as consistently realistic and honest as this is," said Scott Wolf. "I'm proud that we have the kind of show that once people find it, they're hooked. It's borderline scary how involved they get with these characters."

After the trials and tribulations of the first couple of years, the show's success was a true vindication for cast and crew, who'd put everything into it, and fully committed themselves to it.

But even loyal fans seemed to think there was way too much drama going on in the show's fourth season, as crisis piled upon crisis for every member of the family—for everyone, in fact. That was why, after Charlie had beaten his cancer, the producers finally decided to offer some contrast and lighten up a bit.

"The tone of the last episodes will be much different because, post-cancer, there will be a sense of renewed possibilities," announced co-creator Christopher Keyser.

As one of the most popular characters, Sarah Reeves would be heavily featured, of course, and her relationship with Bailey, for the moment platonic, would be explored. And there'd be more for Sarah: getting out in the world, finding a new romance. But would she and Bailey ever get back together, as so many viewers hoped?

In some episodes Sarah barely seemed to figure, as the storylines focused on other people, but for Love that was perfect, since she had two movies to make, even as the show was filming. She was stretched thin enough as it was, without having to give even more time to Sarah. Although she had no wish to give up the character, she loved Sarah, and *Party of Five,* too much. So she went without sleep and pushed herself to the limit in order to do everything: working on the show, filming *Can't Hardly Wait* (which was then known as *The Party*), then the small independent film *Telling You.* She was able to fit in a much-needed two-week break in Hawaii over Christmas, but that was the only vacation she had. And then ABC came knocking, asking her to host a special called *The Senior Prom,* which was ironic, since she'd never had the chance to really go to one of her own (except when she was living in Hawaii, filming *Byrds of Paradise,* and one of the extras invited her to his). She had, to all intents and purposes, become a teen icon.

Love was willing to give people a little peek into the future, namely that "Sarah moves in with Bailey, but they're just friends—for now. Actually this season, they're both going to have a romantic relationship with somebody else ... [T]he way we've been playing it so far [Sarah's new relationship will be] pretty darned free. She's really fallen head over feet for this guy. But I don't know if it's to make Bailey jealous or if it's something she truly feels."

It was Sarah and Bailey who once more kicked off the new season. Although Sarah hadn't been hurt too badly when Bailey had crashed his Jeep the season before, that wasn't enough for Mr. Reeves. He had Bailey charged with drunken driving, although Sarah pleaded with him just to let things be. She told Bailey that she was even willing to lie in court, commit perjury, to get him off, but he knew he couldn't let her do that—it would go totally against her principles.

If he decided to fight, the family would be required to mortgage the house in order to pay for a lawyer. And, he knew, the simple truth was that he *had* been drunk. So, in the end, he pleaded guilty, to make things easier for everyone, and to be honest. He was sentenced to probation, assigned to do community service, and lost his license. Mr. Reeves had extracted his revenge. Sarah, though, was disgusted at her father, so much so that she packed her things and left home.

Sarah's family might have come from money, but that didn't make her less naïve than anyone else. Instead she seemed more naïve than most. She had no street smarts, and soon found herself ripped off by a crooked landlord in her apartment. With his new criminal record,

Bailey was finding it impossible to get a job. He and Sarah decided to combine forces—purely platonically—and become the managers of an apartment building, mostly to take advantage of the free apartment that came with the job. For now, it was a situation that suited them both, except for the strange tenant in number 14 who kept demanding maintenance service. The tenant was Annie Mott (Paige Turco), who had a daughter named Natalie (Allison Bertolino). But they began viewing Annie a little differently when Bailey saw her at an AA meeting. Talking to her, Bailey discovered she had financial problems. When he started giving her money out of the cookie jar he and Sarah used to keep *their* money in, Sarah wasn't too happy.

Annie was interested in Bailey, and once she learned that he and Sarah weren't a couple, she made the first move on him. He would have responded, except his AA sponsor disapproved of the idea.

Sarah, meanwhile, had begun dating Elliott (Christopher Gorham), much to Bailey's dismay, and she believed she was ready to lose her virginity, only to discover that, without loving someone, she simply couldn't do it. Once she told Bailey, he became so freaked, his love for Sarah still bubbling just below the surface, that he defied his sponsor and slept with Annie—as usual, for all the wrong reasons.

Then Charlie told the family that he'd been diagnosed as having Hodgkin's disease, and began radiation treatment. It was the beginning of a very rough period, for no one knew if Charlie would survive.

For Sarah too it wasn't an easy time. She had to take a job she hated, in order to make ends meet, because she wasn't getting any money from her family, and school tuition had to be paid.

Bailey had begun managing Salinger's, since Charlie was physically incapable, and he proved excellent at the job, although he found himself forced to fire Julia, who was a rather incompetent waitress.

As Charlie slowly began to recover, he began to get in touch with parts of himself that he'd forgotten. He helped Sarah with a design project for her theater class, and remembered how much he'd loved design at one point. To some, it seemed as if this could be the beginning of a relationship between Charlie and Sarah, but that was never in the cards. If it was going to be anyone in the Salinger family for her, it would be Bailey.

Things looked as if they might be starting to get back onto an even keel for the Salinger family. Until Claudia, unable to deal with Charlie's illness, and thinking everyone was focusing on him, and ignoring her, began playing hooky from school. When her teacher demanded a conference with her and one of her parents, it was Claudia alone who showed up, prompting the teacher to call in the Department of Social Services. They briefly took Claudia and Owen away from the Salinger house, until the situation was sorted out.

Could things have got any worse?

The answer was yes. Right before the first anniversary of his sobriety, Bailey started drinking again. The pressure of running Salinger's while trying to go to school, as well as coping with Annie, was getting to him. He and Annie had told Natalie that they were seeing each other, and she hadn't taken the news too well—so poorly, in fact, that Annie had begun drinking again, herself, and was forced to go into rehab.

That left Sarah and Bailey to look after Natalie, something neither of them had expected or really had the time for—but they did the very best they could. Being around Bailey so much was making Sarah realize that her feelings for him hadn't vanished at all. They were as strong as they'd always been; she'd merely been repressing them. And it became apparent that she didn't have a future with Elliott when he came out as gay. In fact, she began to wonder if she'd die with her virginity intact, ending up as an old spinster. She wasn't having any luck with the men she liked.

When Annie came out of rehab, she began talking to Sarah about her problems, and about Bailey. At the same time, Bailey was talking to Sarah about *his* problems and about Annie. Finally, instead of continuing as their messenger and advisor, she made them sit down with each other and try to sort things out directly.

Bailey did find one solution to his stress. He dropped out of college to concentrate on running the restaurant. There was just no way he could juggle everything otherwise. And, he believed, it would give him more time for Annie, to whom he still felt very close.

Then Annie's ex-husband appeared, wanting to bring the family together again. Bailey's emotional world seemed to be collapsing once more, especially since Sarah had found a new, male roommate. Unsure of what to do, he went where he knew he'd be secure and welcome—to Sarah. Finally, she was able to admit out loud that she loved him, and always had, even during the worst times. They ended up sleeping together, and Sarah lost her virginity.

After all the trauma and despair everyone got what they wanted, which was Sarah and Bailey in each other's arms again. The big question was, How long could it last? He was with her largely on the rebound, even if he did honestly love Sarah.

Even the cast didn't know much in advance what was going to happen. Toward the end of the season, when asked, the best answer Love could offer was, "The one thing I can give away . . . is that we are getting ready to start shooting today the episode before our last and in this episode we don't get back together . . . I haven't heard anything about it so I'm thinking maybe not this season."

However, she did admit that "I don't know *when* it

will happen but I think that everybody knows that we'll have to get back together for I don't know how long, but at some point they're gonna have to get back together. They're just meant to *be*."

She found it hilarious—all the cast did—that a number of viewers would even raise the possibility of a relationship between Sarah and Charlie, when it was never intended to be anything more than platonic.

"So many people thought that," she said. "It was a huge thing. And all I did was deliver Charlie banana bread! I think that's because when a female and a male do something nice for each other [he had helped her with her school project], people automatically assume that something's going on between them. It's funny, because when we filmed that scene, we were joking about it. We were kidding. But when the episode aired and everyone made such a big deal about it, I said, 'Oh, my God, maybe we sent bad vibes out into the universe.'"

It had been a long, draining season for everyone in the cast, although Love, with her schedule so tight it couldn't be squeezed any more, perhaps suffered more than the others. But Matthew Fox, who had to spend a good part of the season getting himself "to that place where Charlie would be feeling nauseated and sick all the time," the end of filming came as a relief, since "there was the whole emotional aspect of it, too, which is obviously really exhausting; you have to get yourself there twelve, fourteen hours a day."

But that was his job, and he'd managed it very well; they all had. More than that, they'd become one of FOX's flagship shows for quality television, with the ratings increasing every week. The show had become something almost unique, an intelligent drama aimed at teens that also appealed to a broad audience. People knew about *Party of Five*, even those who'd never watched it. It had recognition now, and respect, two things which couldn't be bought.

And that meant recognition for the cast, too. It was getting harder for Love to go to the mall or McDonald's without being noticed, but she didn't mind. Without her fans, she fully realized, she wouldn't be on a show that was doing well, or had a bona fide hit movie. She owed them her time, her autograph, her genuine friendliness.

Being in the spotlight did have its downside, however, as when a certain tabloid published a picture of her and said, "It's obvious that Jennifer Love Hewitt is hiding a *Party of Five* in her skirt." Not only was it obviously untrue, it was uncalled for and completely irresponsible. That was enough to make her cry, and quite understandably.

But with no scandal in her life, the tabloids didn't have much material. She wasn't seen around Los Angeles, drinking underage in bars, hanging all over guys. That wasn't what she'd do, anyway, and even if she'd wanted to, there simply wasn't the time. The more she worked, the more work came her way. She was, really, a workaholic, but one who was doing something she absolutely loved. And there was nothing wrong with that, although sleeping became something of a hobby, rather than a regular experience. Love could handle that, though. Easily.

Chapter Eleven

Filming *Can't Hardly Wait* was inevitably a complete stretch on Love's time. She was still in the middle of shooting the current *Party of Five* season, so her schedule had to be juggled to the point where she barely had a second to spare. Once again she had to sleep in the car as she was driven between sets. The part of Amanda, however, was one she felt she just couldn't turn down—the perfect cheerleader, in what was, essentially, a John Hughes film for the nineties. And she'd loved all those John Hughes flicks so much that she just *had* to take part in this film.

"They stopped making the teen romances. This one came along and it was really, really funny and really sweet and the romance in it was just adorable and I loved it a lot."

And, in spite of all the stress, it turned out to be a great experience for her.

"It was really fun," she said. "The directors were great, the cast was wonderful, getting to work with a lot of different people, and my character is somebody I've never played before. She's such a dream girl: perfect hair, perfect makeup, perfect outfit, perfect everything. I've never gotten to do that. I always play the all-American girl next door, super-natural kind of thing."

One thing that appealed to her about Amanda was that the character wasn't simply a bimbo.

"That's the great thing about her. She's the most popular, really... perfect for this guy, and she's really smart; she's not conceited. People think she is, because they always see what's on the outside, but she's actually very nice, and she's got goals, and she just wants to find, like, her one true love."

The film, which had the working title *The Party*, was written and directed by Deborah Kaplan and Harry Elfont, who'd also written *A Very Brady Sequel*, and it deliberately took its cue from eighties films.

"We felt like nobody was making those good John Hughes comedies anymore," said Elfont. This being the nineties, the subject of alcohol had to be touched upon, but only two of the characters drank. Still, scenes had to be cut for the film to end up with the PG-13 rating it needed.

The movie also gave Love a chance at something she'd never experienced—high school parties. She'd never been to one, always having been too busy, and something of a social outsider at school, but she could still empathize.

"Being a teenager is being a teenager," she explained. "I just pictured myself as an eighteen-year-old at a party, and there I was—an eighteen-year-old at a party."

The characters were representative of the usual high school standbys—the jock, the cheerleading prom queen, the stoners and nerds—all gathered together to celebrate the end of four years.

For most of the film, Love stuck to one outfit, and that was quite deliberate.

"We had two separate fittings. What we decided to do was dress my character in one color throughout the entire movie. Even when I finally do change outfits, I'm still wearing blue. We gave her the blue color as sort of a symbolic thing; she sort of feels in a blue mood, she's got a certain sadness about her. One, she's finally allowing herself to be the insecure person that she is. Two, her boyfriend's broken up with her. And, three, because she wants to find true love."

To make Love into the perfect teen queen, the costumers also added hair extensions, and long, false nails, "quite a bit more glamorous than *Party of Five*."

Although Love really had very little in common with Amanda Beckett, she was still able to relate to her character.

"I think the one thing Amanda and I have in common is she's someone, when people look at her, they perceive as one thing, and that's the way they treat her when actually, if they got to know her, she would be something completely different . . . The one thing I tried to bring to Amanda is that understanding that I have of what that's like."

She firmly believed that *Can't Hardly Wait* could be for her generation what *The Breakfast Club* or *Pretty in Pink* or *Sixteen Candles* had been to another generation.

"I think it has that potential—it will be one of those movies that'll come out and do very well . . . it'll be in people's video libraries, and [they'll watch it] when they feel like they want to laugh and sort of fall in love."

A big part of its appeal, Love felt, was that "It's a very real human movie. To me, just being a teenager and being in high school is about that first day when you walk in and people look at you." You are immediately categorized and it becomes almost impossible to break out of it. "And that's where you spend the rest of your four years there. I think that all the people at the party are in their groups, and I think the one thing they realize is that maybe there shouldn't really be a group, that there's really no need for it—they're all kind of the same. They're insecure, they haven't figured out life yet, they're all out of high school, and they're all at a party to have a really good time. I think that the directors did a great thing by writing all those dynamics, and showing all the insecurities of those people."

Love did relate enough to Amanda, however, that she took Amanda's cheerleading trophy home as a souvenir from the set, "because I always wanted to be a cheerleader. I'm such a waste of a great cheerleader."

As soon as the class graduated from Huntington Hills High, after one of those achingly awful ceremonies, everyone got down to the really important things—specifically, the party that night to celebrate the end of high school.

For Amanda Beckett (Love), however, it wasn't going to be fun. Right after graduation, her big-deal jock boyfriend, Mike (Peter Facinelli) had dumped her, to everyone's amazement, and, in some cases, glee. He wanted to be free for all the college women in his future, only to be told during the evening, by Amanda's cousin Ron, that reality was going to be a little different: jocks were a dime a dozen in college.

Preston (Ethan Embry), a nerd and aspiring writer, had been in love with Amanda since the first day of high school, but he'd never had the courage to say anything about it. His infatuation had never vanished, and now, since he was leaving for a writing workshop in Boston the next day, he had his chance to tell her. His way of doing it was to give her a letter he'd written for her. But Amanda was in the middle of a crisis. She'd believed Mike was her true love; she'd defined herself as his girlfriend. Now that they were no longer together, who exactly was she? She needed to find out.

Denise (Lauren Ambrose) was Preston's best friend, and the alienated one in the class, petulant and post-punk with her orange hair and attitude. She and Kenny (Seth Green), who was something of a white, middle-class homeboy, had been friends as kids, but had become distant during high school. A long session in the bathroom gave them a chance to really come to terms with each other.

It was your typical high school party. A wasted stoner licked a slice of watermelon. The Yearbook Girl (Melissa Joan Hart in a cameo performance) was on a mission to have *everyone* sign her yearbook, no matter what they wrote. People drank and let themselves get weird, like the computer geek, William (Charlie Korsmo), who ended up singing Guns N' Roses' "Paradise City."

Amanda and Preston were two complete opposites, the nerd and the queen, but they were the real focus. Amanda wanted to love and be loved, she wanted the real thing. Preston was in love with her. It seemed an unlikely match, but as the movie progressed, they edged inevitably closer and closer together, and Amanda discovered that she didn't have to live her life through someone else's glory, that she could be happy finding out who she really was, and enjoying someone who loved her as she was.

The reviewers weren't too kind to *Can't Hardly Wait*. To adults, all this had been done before, although they seemed to forget that for this generation, it was something new, something about them and their peers. *Entertainment Weekly* dismissed the characters as existing "entirely in prepackaged pop-culture boxes. They're recombinant youth-movie clichés, the majority of them derived from those glorious ancient days of the mid-to-late '80s," and concluded that the film was "agreeably mindless generation-next trash, but it leaves you hungry for a movie in which the characters are more than walking screenwriter index cards."

Variety was a little more thoughtful, but hardly more encouraging, calling it "a comedy that's neither authentic in its lingo and concerns nor universal enough to appeal to broader segments of the audience; it succeeds only partially in conveying the excitement, fear, and confusion of that momentous night when adolescence ends and young adulthood begins." The reviewer, Emanuel Levy, was willing to concede that "sporadically, the writing is good . . . pacing in first segments is frantic, later sequences, though, are more sensitive, helping to bring out some acute observations in the more intimate interactions."

Other than saying that the leads were "charming," *Variety* made no mention of Love's performance, while *Entertainment Weekly* was only lukewarm: "Hewitt, with her wistful Lily Tomlin dimples, is very sweet, but in this movie she has more hair than personality."

What the reviewers handily chose to forget was that high school never really changes. There, as later in life, people fall into stereotypes. It was as if that had been okay during their youth, but now things should have moved on, and that really wasn't going to happen. *Can't Hardly Wait* wasn't going to win any Oscars, but that had never been its aim. It offered a portrait of a time and place that would resonate with a lot of people. The characters might have been drawn with fairly wide brushstrokes, but that made them all the more accessible and identifiable to audiences. The film had comedy and romance in fairly equal doses, and exactly the kind of happy ending it needed to succeed. Certainly the opinion of the critics was disregarded by the people the film was aimed at. In its first weekend alone, *Can't Hardly Wait* took in $8 million, which came close to covering the $10 million budget, and within two months it had grossed well over $24 million—hardly a failure!

After filming one movie alongside her work on *Party of Five*, Love should have needed a break of some kind. But that simply wasn't in the cards for her; she was far too much in demand. The offers were stacking up like planes at a busy airport.

There was a short break over Christmas, when Love

did allow herself a few days to get away to Hawaii and just relax. No sooner had she returned, though, than she was shuttling between the character of Sarah Reeves on TV and Deb Friedman in yet another new film, *Telling You*, which was to be released in the late summer of 1998.

That kind of pressure would have broken a lot of people, but Love was barely getting started. While she'd never had any ambitions to direct a film herself, the idea of being a producer definitely appealed to her, and she quite literally dreamed up the possibility of becoming one with *Cupid's Love*.

The story came to her one night as she was sleeping.

"I woke up and went, 'Wow, part of what I dreamed would be a really cool movie.' For most people that would have been the end of the story. That day, though, Love was traveling, and on the plane she wrote a film treatment of her dream, calling it *Cupid's Love*. It was the story of a wedding planner who fell in love with one of her clients, a groom-to-be.

When Love described her idea to her family, both Pat and Tood Hewitt were enthusiastic, so she took the next step, registering the title and idea with the Writers Guild, so no one could steal it. A couple of days later she met some friends in the business who were scouting around for new film properties, and Love said, " 'Well, the crazy thing is I just wrote this treatment for this thing and do you guys mind hearing me just tell you the story?' I said, 'I cannot pitch, like, to save my life. I'm not any good at this, I've never done this before but do you mind me, like, telling you the story to see if you like it or not?' And they were like, 'No, sure, go ahead, blah blah blah.' So I went on ahead and I tell them the story and they loved it and they're like, 'Let's try and make it happen.' "

That started the ball rolling, but much of the work, of talking to the studios, had to come from Love herself, since she was not only going to be the writer, but also the producer and star of the film—if she could convince anyone to put up the money for it to be made.

And so she had to talk to different studios, to keep on pitching her idea. For that job, she decided to look the part of a producer, putting on a suit, and even a pair of wire-rimmed glasses, although she didn't need them.

"I'm an actress," she explained. "I know how to dress for the role and adopt the right attitude. I want to look serious so the studio people will take me seriously."

It took some time, and was incredibly nerve-wracking for Love, but in the end her efforts were rewarded.

"It was more important for me to earn the respect of the studio executives than to sell my idea. And they gave it to me, which was nice. But I've never been so exhausted in my life."

She also walked away a great deal richer, as New Line paid her $500,000 just for the treatment. Her salary for starring in the film, which was shot during the summer of 1998, would come on top of that. And she'd also be seeing her name on the credits as a producer.

"The only reason I wanted to [produce] in the first place is because I feel like my part of filmmaking is so small. I get to come in and do my part after everybody else has done theirs. They get the exciting part—they get to be there for the meetings, and put the characters together. I just get to play it after they're done. I want so badly to be a bigger part of the [creative process]."

Not that she wasn't happy with acting, but she was still discovering herself, spreading her wings. And it was definitely taking her places.

One place she was certainly going as soon as the season of *Party of Five* wrapped was the set of *I Still Know What You Did Last Summer*, the sequel to her box office smash.

Work began on April 20, 1998, with Love returning as Julie James. The only other original cast member reprising a role was Freddie Prinze, Jr., coming back as Ray. Brandy, the R&B hitmaker and star of the TV show *Moesha*, had also signed to make her first feature film. One person who wouldn't be a direct part of this project was writer Kevin Williamson.

"Kevin is so busy doing like forty other things," Love explained. "The idea was his. When he wrote *I Know What You Did Last Summer*, he wrote the treatment for the second one."

Much of it would take place in the Bahamas, although the locations were actually filmed in Mexico, to save money. But one thing it wouldn't be was a cheesy rip-off of the original.

"It's terrifying," she said. "It's so good, that it could stand on its own, and never have had the first one. It's excellent."

The script might even have been scarier than the first one. When Love read it, she was "so terrified" that she had to sleep in the same bed as her mother that night.

She didn't want Julie to be exactly the same as she'd been in the original movie. Her character would have grown and changed, and she wanted that to be reflected in the script.

"The one thing I hate about sequels is that the lead character is always the same person. So I made sure Julie was different this time."

How different? That remained to be seen, and Love wasn't about to give away any secrets. All she'd say, jokingly, was, "I'll be back. I'll be in pain [from the final shower scene], because that thing *hurt*, I gotta tell ya. But I shall scream again."

She was willing to reveal that Julie would look a little different. She'd be buff, because Love herself had been working out, but Julie was "gonna wear dark, smoky eye makeup, baggy pants, and short T-shirts."

And it was every bit as physical a shoot as the first, with Love often coming home from the studio covered in bumps and bruises, with lots of fake blood under her fingernails.

Once again, Love was to be the star, although Brandy's name would undoubtedly lure more than a few people into the theaters, too. But Jennifer Love Hewitt had become a major name, a big deal, both on television and in the movies. At nineteen, she was a force to be reckoned with, but really just beginning to gather momentum.

"The only thing success has done is that it's made me realize I could be having more fun by taking roles that are a little different. Maybe it would be fun to find a movie to play a character that is completely opposite from me and take some chances and dye my hair purple, if that's what it calls for. Or cut my hair off short. Just do things like that... I think it would be fun to do something really different. Not necessarily raunchy... but just different... Maybe like a bad girl, like somebody that causes a little trouble."

But there was also a side of her that yearned to play romantic comedies, like *Sleepless in Seattle* or *While You Were Sleeping*.

There was no likelihood of her leaving *Party of Five* for greener and richer pastures in the movie business, though. The show was happily renewed for a fifth season by FOX, and Love had every intention of being there as Sarah for as long as they wanted her.

She understood just how much she owed to her character, what playing Sarah had brought her in terms of recognition and artistic satisfaction, and the door the exposure had opened for her. Without any doubt she was well enough known to have left, to have gone solo and pursued a movie career but why would she want to leave something she absolutely loved?

* * *

Nowadays her schedule has become totally crazed. She has enough to do to fill every waking hour, and there's plenty more she could do if she had the time. There's barely time to relax, let alone have an evening with friends or take a drive down to Color Me Mine and paint some ceramics. This is what she's spent the last ten years working for, however, this success, being in demand this way, and her happiness is reflected in her attitude. She *wants* to do everything, or at least every possible thing she has the time for, without sacrificing any quality.

"There are gonna be times when you're completely overwhelmed and unable to handle things no matter what you do. You just gotta say, 'Today, this is my life, and whatever it's gonna make me—mad, sad, or happy—I have to embrace it. That was my life for today.' When you think too much, sometimes it's like you miss it."

Sarah Reeves has made her who she is, and she's grateful that it's happened that way. Those other series, even though they didn't work out in the long term, prepared her for the big one. They gave her the experience of working as an actress, honed her professionalism, and let her know that yes, she really could do this.

And she did, perhaps, have the very best role, getting close to a hottie like Scott Wolf, particularly when "he's a good kisser."

More than that, she's been involved with one of the best shows in television this decade, and it means so much to her to have that association, even if girls have come up to her, claiming that because of her they've changed their names to Sarah on their birth certificates.

Both on and off the screen she's become a role model for girls, and that's a responsibility she takes very seriously. It's one of the reasons she'd never play a druggie or someone whose character was *too* far removed from her own. And it's one of the reasons she continues to live a very normal life, going to the store to rent videos, painting at Color Me Mine, eating at McDonald's—all the things a normal girl her age would do. She's successful, but it hasn't turned her head. Her eyes might be on the sky, but her feet are firmly planted on the ground. She has a remarkably strong and vivid sense of herself and her place in the overall scheme of things.

The way things have gone, it would be excusable if her ego got the better of her at times, but that's never happened. She's never been the prima donna; instead, she's the cool and collected professional who juggles all her commitments, is on the set, prepared, when she's supposed to be, and, like Sarah, puts herself last.

She is, quite simply, a lovely person, who treats others the way she'd like them to treat her. Sometimes, though, people do get her and the characters she plays confused.

"During my first rehearsal for *Can't Hardly Wait*," she recalled, "I was practicing a scene where I'm being mean. When I was done, this extra, who didn't realize I was acting, came up to me and said, 'I thought you were that nice girl from *Party of Five*. I can't believe that you would treat your fellow actors the way you did.' I was so embarrassed because I couldn't convince him that I was acting."

The fact that she would even try to convince him, rather than blow it off, says volumes about her. And someone who's willing to go to those lengths, a star willing to be that human, has a long and glittering career ahead of her.

Chapter Twelve

Being successful in one career is hard enough. Juggling two careers has to be close to impossible, but Love manages it. To be fair, she's not actively pursuing her singing at present, since there isn't the time to focus on it properly. But in its place she's become a movie producer and writer, both of which carry plenty of responsibility, and she's promised that when *Cupid's Love* is made, she'll be contributing to its soundtrack.

For someone who's barely twenty, she's achieved a remarkable amount. And she's done it all while keeping her integrity, her moral center. Many who are eager to make it in television or movies are willing to do anything. Instead, she's always been involved in series that have had quality, rather than diving for the lowest common denominator. In movies, she's always been certain that she would never do a nude scene, and buy into that kind of exploitation. Indeed, she has been offered plenty of parts that she wouldn't even consider.

"I feel because my character on *Party of Five* is such a role model, I have a responsibility when I take other roles not to stray too far. I don't want to be somebody who for three years has played this person who's a strong, amazing person, and then go off over the summer to play some psychotic drug addict. It's too schizo for me. I wouldn't want teenagers to think I was saying that's okay. But even if it wasn't a role model, I don't think I would play those kind of roles."

Love has said several times that at some point she'd like to go to college, possibly to Stanford, where she could study child psychology, with the eventual aim of writing children's books. It might seem an odd ambition for someone who already has an amazing career, but everyone has goals.

She's actually already become a published author, having contributed an essay to the best-selling *Chicken Soup for the Teenage Soul,* a piece that came out of her involvement with Tuesday's Child, a pediatric AIDS organization, which is just one of several of Love's charitable interests. The editors of the book approached her because Sarah Reeves is such a teen role model, and Love was more than happy to give them something for a book aimed specifically at teens, her peer group.

"When they're feeling down or feeling like things in their life are not that great, they can read the book and know there are other teenagers who actually have it a little worse than they do," she said.

Along with another contributor, Kimberly Kirberger, she hosted a book signing for *Chicken Soup for the Teenage Soul* at the Motown Cafe in Las Vegas in September 1997, where she was inundated with requests for autographs. It was, perhaps, an apt place to launch the book, since back in the sixties, Tamla Motown Records had called itself "The Sound of Young America." Love played up the connection by wearing heels, a silver dress, and a blond bouffant wig (she's often said she'll take height any way she can get it!). And, of course, there was dancing, lots of it, along with Love doing a version of the Martha and the Vandellas oldie, "Dancing in the Streets."

Given her status, it was perhaps inevitable that she'd be approached to become a spokesperson for some product, and indeed, that was the case. In March 1998, she signed to become the voice and face of Neutrogena, replacing former MTV VJ Martha Quinn. Love was asked, according to Neutrogena's marketing director, because she's "vibrant and upbeat and brings a lot of energy to the products." Needless to say, it didn't hurt that "she also has great skin."

That was a first for Love, and it was a very clear sign of just how far she'd come. No longer was she just an actress. She was a star, a celebrity in her own right. In April 1998 she did a reading for *Blood and Chocolate,* an upcoming MGM feature film about a female werewolf who falls for a man. Whether she ended up taking the role or not, it was a case of the studio coming to her. She no longer had to audition. That was also the case with an upcoming TV movie about Audrey Hepburn, which was to feature Love portraying one of her great screen idols. Jennifer Love Hewitt had become a power in the young Hollywood, as evidenced by the money she'd been given to develop *Cupid's Love.*

While it may seem that success is just piling on success for her these days, it's worth remembering that she's worked long and hard to reach this point. She may have made it look easy, moving from one show to another, but each part required a lot of dedication. And at the root of it all were two things: a desire within her to make it happen, and a whole load of talent.

It would be impossible to forget that she couldn't have done it without her mother, Pat Hewitt.

"Mom is a big reason why Love is who she is," Todd Hewitt said of his family, and it's true. Very few parents would have been willing to put their own careers on hold in order to take off for Hollywood and pursue the wild dreams of a ten-year-old. But, as Pat explained, "I thought everybody's little girl could do what she did."

Of course, that's obviously not true, or every girl *would* be doing it. It requires dedication and sacrifice

Love may not regret bypassing a normal adolescence, but most teens aren't as driven as she is. They want the social thing, the parties, the high school cliques, all the normal experiences. She hasn't had the girlfriends a normal girl would have, the same chances for gossip and crushing.

From the first she's been totally professional. It was one of the things that impressed the people at *Party of Five* when she was first cast as Sarah Reeves. "Love has a seventeen-year-old's personality and a grownup's professional perspective," commented executive producer Chistopher Keyser at the time.

While her career may seem to have just zoomed straight up, there have been plenty of disappointments along the way. Series were canceled or never picked up. Records went largely unpromoted, and so never sold.

There was even the personal heartbreak of being dumped by boyfriends, when "you can't breathe, your eyes are pouring a thousand tears a second, and you can't foresee going on in the love department because you never want to feel this way again." But that passed, and for a little over two years she and Will Friedle were ridiculously happy together.

"One of my favorite things to do is kiss Will," she once said. "It's the only thing better than chocolate."

Unfortunately, the taste seemed to sour, as they eventually broke up. Typically, it happened out of the spotlight, remaining a private matter to be resolved between themselves, not for public consumption. The first anyone realized, in fact, was when Love was seen around town with MTV's Carson Daly, a hunk himself, and it became obvious that the two of them were more than just good friends.

She's slowly spreading her wings, but is in no hurry to flap them completely. Living with her mom works fine; it removes some of the responsibility she'd have in a place of her own. She doesn't feel the need to grow up completely yet. It's only in the last year that she's learned to drive.

She's splurged and bought herself a navy-blue Land Rover Discovery, which might be the perfect vehicle for negotiating the L.A. freeways.

"My mom taught me how to drive," she explained. "But it's a pain being in the car with her. When she's with me it's 'Oooooh! Uuuggh! Waaaatch!' It's not driving that makes me nervous, it's all of her noises! Whenever she gets in the car, I just turn up the stereo so I can't hear her and I'm fine."

That may sound a little brutal, but the relationship Love and Pat share has always been special and close. Her mom and her brother keep her grounded, although that's something she hardly needs. Jennifer Love Hewitt has learned from everything she's done. She knows how to play the Hollywood game without getting wrapped up in the hype. When she appeared on the *Tonight* show, the biggest thing she could think of was that her grandmother loved to watch it—hardly the thoughts of someone who considers herself a "star."

And that may be her secret. Her face may appear on television every week, she may play the lead in movies, but underneath all that she's a very real person who enjoys the ordinary things in life, who loves her family, who likes to go to the mall or to McDonald's and be as normal as the next girl. That's healthy, especially for someone who has so much going for her, who can do whatever she wants.

"She is talented, beautiful and sings like an angel," Jamie Lee Curtis once said of her. "She has the tools to do whatever she wants."

The future is wide open for her. Acting, singing, producing, writing, she can do it all. But she's in no rush to embrace everything at once. Neve Campbell may have made noises about leaving *Party of Five* to follow a movie career; Love is in no hurry at all to abandon

Sarah for brighter lights. She thinks things through, deals with everything in a deliberate way.

For the moment, in movies she's concentrating on teen films, since that's where her real audience lies. But as she and her fans grow, that will change. Love has it in her to become one of the biggest actresses of her generation, to make a smooth transition to the adult dramatic and comedic roles and sustain a long and happy career.

She just has so much going for her, because she's already done so much. *I Know What You Did Last Summer* pushed her into the young blockbuster class. Its sequel will simply confirm her status there, while *Cupid's Love* will add the producer's arrow to her bow.

It's all spread out ahead of her, and you know it's all going to happen for her, because she wants it to, and because she's willing to put in the work to *make* it happen, and has the talent to back it all up.

Unassuming, lovely, a very genuine person, she deserves every bit of success that comes her way. Love deserves love, and that's what she seems to have found.

Twenty, thirty years from now, Sarah Reeves will be little more than a memory, or she may show up on a dusty rerun on an obscure cable channel. But Jennifer Love Hewitt will still be vibrant, flourishing in her careers, whatever they may be by then, still taking on the world and winning, with her head on straight, perhaps raising a family, and always retaining her ability to make things happen.

She's made a smooth transition from child actor to teen actor, and the change to adult will be every bit as silky. She's called herself "the girl next door," but there are very few like her living next door to most people. She's got it going on, and it's not going to stop anytime soon.

As Sarah/Julie/Amanda, or whoever, Jennifer Love Hewitt is still there underneath it all, with the intelligence, wit, and personality to propel her characters. She's made her own success, she's living her own life on her own terms. She's happy and totally fulfilled. And, really, what more can anyone ask from life than that?

She's got it all. And she always will have.

Love on the Web

Love is one of the most accessed female stars on the Web, and as she gets bigger, that's going to explode, not that it already hasn't. There are a few lame sites, and there are some that are extraordinary. This is a selection of the very best.

http://www.LoveHewitt.com might just be the ultimate unofficial site. Lots of pictures, transcripts of articles, plus all the breaking news about Love that anyone could want, updated very regularly. Fan sites really don't come any better than this.

http://w3.ime.net/akira/jlh_index.htm takes you to Akira's really impressive site. Strong on the visuals, and there are *lots* of them, enough to satisfy anyone.

http://www.stuweeks.u-net.com/ is the home of the Bailey and Sarah Online Fan Club, with episode synopses, reviews, pictures, interviews, and lots of fan input.

There are plenty of *Party of Five* sites, but for once the official one has to be among the best. Point that browser at *http://www.foxworld.com/po5/* right now!

Jennifer Love Hewitt—Credits

Television Series

Kids Incorporated
. . . as Robin

Running Wilde **(pilot, never aired)**

Shaky Ground
. . . as Bernadette Moody

Byrds of Paradise
. . . as Franny Byrd

McKenna
. . . as Cassidy McKenna

Party of Five
. . . as Sarah Reeves

Television Specials

True Tales of Teen Trauma (MTV, 1996)
Hosted by Love

FOX Halloween Bash (FOX, 1996)
Filmed in Florida, Love was a featured performer

The Senior Prom (ABC, 1997)
Documentary hosted by Love

Video

Dance! Workout With Barbie (1991)
Love danced and also sang all the songs

Trojan War (aka *Rescue Me*) (1997)
Really a movie, but released directly onto video

Films

Munchie (1992)
Director: Jim Wynorski
Loni Anderson . . . Cathy
Andrew Stevens . . . Elliott
Arte Johnson . . . Prof. Cruikshank
Dom DeLuise . . . Munchie (voice)
Love Hewitt . . . Andrea

Little Miss Millions (aka *Home for Christmas*) (1993)

Director: Jim Wynorski
Love Hewitt . . . Heather Lofton
Howard Hesseman . . . Nick Frost
Anita Morriss . . . Sybil Lofton
James Avery . . . Noah Hollander
Steve Landesburg . . . Harvey Lipschitz

Sister Act II: Back in the Habit (1993)

Director: Bill Duke
Whoopi Goldberg . . . Deloris
Kathy Najimy . . . Sister Mary Patrick
Barnard Hughes . . . Father Maurice
James Coburn . . . Mr. Crisp
Jennifer ``Love'' Hewitt . . . Margaret

House Arrest (1996)

Director: Harry Winer
Kyle Howard . . . Grover Beindorf
Russel Harper . . . TJ Krupp
Jamie Lee Curtis . . . Janet Beindorf
Kevin Pollak . . . Ned Beindorf
Jennifer Tilly . . . Cindy Figler
Jennifer Love Hewitt . . . Brooke Figler

Trojan War (1997)

Director: George Huang
Will Friedle . . . Brad

Marley Shelton . . . Brooke
Jennifer Love Hewitt . . . Leah
Eric Balfour . . . Kyle
Lee Majors . . . Officer Austin

I Know What You Did Last Summer (1997)

Director: Jim Gillespie
Jennifer Love Hewitt . . . Julie James
Sarah Michelle Gellar . . . Helen Shivers
Ryan Phillippe . . . Barry Cox
Freddie Prinze, Jr. . . . Ray Bronson
Muse Watson . . . Benjamin Willis

Can't Hardly Wait (1998)

Director: Harry Elfont and Deborah Kaplan
Jennifer Love Hewitt . . . Amanda Beckett
Ethan Embry . . . Preston
Peter Facinelli . . . Mike
Seth Green . . . Kenny
Lauren Ambrose . . . Denise

Telling You (1998)

I Still Know What You Did Last Summer (1999)

Cupid's Love (1999)

Discography

Love Songs
(Medlac, Japan, 1992)
FIRST TASTE OF LOVE / BEDTIME STORIES / PLEASE SAVE US THE WORLD / LISTEN (TO YOUR HEART) / WON'T U BE MINE / 90s KIDS / I'LL FIND YOU / DANCING QUEEN / LOVE (WHAT'S IT GONNA TAKE?) / A LITTLE JAZZ / BEN

Let's Go Bang
(Atlantic, U.S., 1995)
KISS AWAY FROM HEAVEN / LET'S GO BANG / DIFFERENCE BETWEEN US / COULDN'T FIND ANOTHER MAN / YOU MAKE ME SMILE / IN ANOTHER LIFE / GARDEN (INTRO) / CAN'T STAND IN THE WAY OF LOVE / FREE TO BE A WOMAN / EVERYWHERE I GO / DON'T TURN YOUR HEAD AWAY / BABY I'M-A WANT YOU

Jennifer Love Hewitt
(Atlantic, U.S., 1996)
COOL WITH YOU / NO ORDINARY LOVE / (OUR LOVE) DON'T THROW IT ALL AWAY / NEVER A DAY GOES BY / DON'T PUSH THE RIVER / THE GREATEST WORD / I WANT A LOVE I CAN SEE / I WAS ALWAYS YOUR GIRL / LAST NIGHT / I BELIEVE IN . . . / NEVER A DAY GOES BY (ACOUSTIC VERSION) / IT'S GOOD TO KNOW I'M ALIVE